Build Your Own
High-Performance
Gamers' Mod PC

About the Authors

Edward S. Chen was raised in Queens, NY and currently resides in Albany, NY. He is a web programmer for AOL/Time Warner, one of the largest media and entertainment companies in the world. Edward designs and maintains database backends for the numerous web ventures in the Albany, NY affiliate.

Edward is also the founder and web master of GideonTech.com. The website is dedicated to case and accessory modifications for the PC. The site receives about one million visits per month from all corners of the globe, and has been mentioned in a number of magazines around the country.

Joel Durham, Jr. was, is, and ever shall be a computer gaming junkie. Joel's second passion is writing. After spending his childhood with a Commodore 64 and having little else to interact with, he broke into his dream job as *PC Gamer's* first technical editor. However, he and his wife were frightened off by the cost of living in the Bay Area where *PC Gamer's* offices reside, so he returned home to the Rochester, NY area to pursue a freelance career. He's written for magazines and web sites including *PC Gamer, Computer Gaming World, Computer Source Magazine, Incite, PC Magazine,* PC Accelerator, Voodoo, GameSpot, Gamecenter, Gamer's Depot, Sharky Extreme, and more.

Build Your Own High-Performance Gamers' Mod PC

Edward Chen
Joel Durham, Jr.

McGraw-Hill/Osborne

New York   Chicago   San Francisco   Lisbon   London   Madrid   Mexico City
Milan   New Delhi   San Juan   Seoul   Singapore   Sydney   Toronto

The McGraw·Hill Companies

McGraw-Hill/Osborne
2100 Powell Street, Floor 10
Emeryville, California 94608
U.S.A.

To arrange bulk purchase discounts for sales promotions, premiums, or fund-raisers, please contact **McGraw-Hill**/Osborne at the above address. For information on translations or book distributors outside the U.S.A., please see the International Contact Information page immediately following the index of this book.

Build Your Own High-Performance Gamers' Mod PC

1234567890 QPD QPD 019876543

ISBN **0-07-222901-2**

Publisher
  Brandon A. Nordin

Vice President & Associate Publisher
  Scott Rogers

Acquisitions Editor
  Francis Kelly

Project Editor
  Monika Faltiss

Acquisitions Coordinator
  Tana Allen

Technical Editor
  Paul Pavlichek

Copy Editor
  Lisa Theobald

Proofreader
  Mike McGee

Indexer
  Jack Lewis

Computer Designers
  Carie Abrew,
  Jean Butterfield, John Patrus

Illustrators
  Melinda Moore Lytle,
  Michael Mueller, Lyssa Wald

Series Design
  Jean Butterfield

Cover Series Design
  Ted Holladay

Cover Illustration
  Ted Holladay

This book was composed with Corel VENTURA™ Publisher.

This book is dedicated to my parents,
Louis and Nora Chen,
who have always supported me
in my every decision in life.
Also to Suzanne Moy
for all the love
and encouragement
these past few years.

—Edward

This book is dedicated to Emily, my darling wife,
who put up with more than any wife should have
during the creation of this book.

—Joel

Contents at a Glance

Contents

Acknowledgments

I would like to thank the following individuals, without their guidance and assistance, this book would not have been published. Thanks to Francis Kelly, editor, all the staff at McGraw-Hill/Osborne, and Paul Pavlichek for the technical corrections. Will, Teann, Kevin, and Uyen, thanks for keeping me grounded and humble. And finally, I want to thank my entire staff and community at GideonTech.com for their constant ideas and input.

—Edward Chen

I would like to thank Intel and AMD for providing me with processors on short notice, Antec for the case, SOYO for the terrific motherboard, and Creative Labs, Philips, and Guillemot for the top notch sound cards. Also, thanks to ATI for the awe inspiring Radeon 9700 Pro, Logitech for the killer speakers, the gamepad, the mouse, and the wheel, and Saitek for the joystick combo. Last but not least, I'd like to thank Matt Firme and *PC Gamer* magazine for giving me my big break as a computer writer

—Joel Durham, Jr.

Introduction

Hardcore gamers are unique among computer users. They're the gear-heads who want bleeding edge performance. They're the bloodhounds who sniff out even the tiniest frame rate improvement. They settle for nothing but the fastest and most powerful PC equipment on the market.

Whether it's you we've just described here, or if you're just a casual gamer who wants to put together a hot new PC with your own bare hands, you've come to your Mecca. *Build Your Own High-Performance Gamers' Mod PC* takes you one step at a time through choosing components and putting a system together, from the case to the motherboard, and the graphics card through the speakers.

There are a number of advantages to building your own PC rather than buying one, even the overpriced but performance heavy systems from houses like Alienware. When you build your own PC, you learn a lot more about computers than you'd learn in any computer science class. You read reviews and do all the research to find parts to your liking, and then surf around some more to learn how to tweak them.

Everything in a hand-built PC is yours. You don't cut corners to shave the bottom line. You decide what's best, and you install it, so you know the job is done with the care and attention it needs. Your PC didn't come off an assembly line in Taiwan, it was lovingly built by you, and you're going to get more out of it than you ever would had you bought a ready-made, branded PC. In this book, we provide you with details of the three most common case modifications you can start on for your case.

When I started on case modifications, there were few guides available to explain what can or cannot be done. Although that was the case back then, it did help open up the underground scene to some insane modifications. With the "sky as the limit" mentality, many modders paved the way to what people are so accustomed to now. There was no set rule as to what you could or could not do, which is what drew a lot of people to the scene. Nowadays, local mom and pop stores and large retailers carry case modification accessories like acrylic windows and lighting products. To say that modification has hit the mainstream is an understatement; it has taken the market by storm.

The second part of this book is split into three chapters, each detailing one specific topic; namely window construction, lighting, and case painting. Modified computer towers with windows and lighting was the first modification I accomplished on my own case a few years ago. With just one tool, I was able to change the way a computer case looked. You know you have created something special when your non-technical friends come over and notice your work. People who normally would not be interested in learning what a CPU is, will start asking you questions about your prized project.

The projects in the chapters are aimed mainly at jump-starting you into case modification. They should not be considered as the absolute standard to follow. Custom modification is so enticing mainly because each person can work on the same case, yet have results that can be drastically different. Do not hold back! Let your imagination take over. If you can picture it in your mind, it can be done. The most exciting part of a project is the end, when you sit back and look at your work. Instead of settling for the factory built "clones," you have just created something different that expresses your personality.

Part I

Making It a High-Performance PC

Chapter 1

The Case and Power Supply

Tools of the Trade

A medium Philips head screwdriver

Two of the most overlooked components of a computer system are the case and power supply. If PCs were people, overlooking those vital parts would be like overlooking our skin and our hearts, respectively; but while we may not think about them very often, they're crucial to our survival.

The case, or chassis, is the conglomeration of metal, plastic, or a combination of both that holds together the computer components. It's the place where you mount the motherboard, power supply, cooling fans, drives, and other components; its cover shields you from the oft-considerable noise a high-performance PC can make; it gives you something to mod to create a unique and individual statement about yourself. (*Mod*, short for modify, is covered in the last three chapters of this book.)

Meanwhile, the power supply gives life to the components in the PC. It regulates and distributes the flow of electricity that makes the processor, sound card, video card, hard drive, and other components come alive. Too often it's considered a secondary component, if it's considered at all, probably because most cases come with power supplies and we take them for granted. However, overloading a cheap, generic power supply can cause damage to the rest of the system, and some power supplies have greater protective capabilities than others.

Throughout this book, it's assumed that you're building a high-performance PC that you plan to keep up-to-date by upgrading components as the originals grow old or as new technologies emerge, and it's also assumed that you plan to mod your case in one way or another to give it some panache that plain beige just doesn't convey.

The Chassis

Your computer's case is where all of the internal peripherals are held. It houses the motherboard, and hence the expansion slots, drive bays, and everything that goes in them. Because this book is all about being a hands-on PC enthusiast, you'll want a chassis that's large enough for plenty of finger room and expansion. Plus, you'll want to consider factors such as its heat conductivity, mod-ability, size, and more.

Selecting a chassis is a decision that's more serious than most people consider. You'll have to live with your decision for a long time. Since you'll be building your computer out of standardized parts, you won't be building a disposable machine that you can toss out in three years for a newer model; you're building a fully upgradable beast that you can keep fresh for as long as you wish. It's all going to live in the case, so don't skimp and buy the cheapest chassis out there.

Of course, cases are, for the most part, as interchangeable as the PC parts themselves, so you're not absolutely stuck on the first case you choose. If you get sick of your case, of if a mod goes bad and you end up with a hunk of shredded sheet metal, you can always replace your case—but it's a labor-intensive process.

Case Selection

Since virtually everything resides in the case itself, swapping one case for another is the most burdensome upgrade you can possibly perform. That's why you should take particular care in selecting a case you can live with for a long time. You should focus on a large, roomy case with plenty of drive bays for future expansion.

Form Factor

The term *form factor* is used frequently throughout this book. Basically, a form factor is the shape, size, and physical specification of a piece of hardware. A 3½-inch, half-height hard drive fits in a 3½-inch bay in your case because each follows its own form factor; that's what makes them compatible. Power supplies fit into cases because they follow the same form factor, making them the right fit for each other.

Through the years, a cornucopia of form factors have been used for computer chassis. These form factors also include the power supply and motherboard, since both components have to fit in the case. The current form factor of choice for cases, power supplies, and motherboards is called ATX, although it's not the only one you might encounter.

Other, older form factors include (but are not limited to) the previously popular AT, the smaller baby-AT, and the LPX. The AT form factor is flexible in that it can accommodate desktop and tower cases of various sizes, much like the current ATX form factor. The baby-AT is shaped around much smaller motherboards, some so small that in the computer shop where I used to work, we called them "credit cards." LPX is quite different from current standards, with a typically flat case with few expansion bays that reside on a riser perpendicular to the motherboard; expansion cards are parallel to the motherboard.

For a high-end gamer's mod PC, you'll definitely want to go with ATX equipment. Your choices in chassis are broad. You'll find cases of different sizes and shapes—flat desktop cases, short mini towers, medium-height mid towers, big full towers, large server cases, and flat rackmount cases. If you're building and modding your first PC, go with a mid tower or full tower, as they're not only the most common cases, but also the most accessible and easiest to mod. Figure 1-1 shows a typical mid-tower ATX case.

Figure 1-1
A typical mid-tower ATX case

Expansion

Another concern in the hunt for the greatest case is its expandability. How many drives can you stuff into it? How easy is it to get them in there? Does it require (shudder) drive rails?

Every case has a certain number of 5¼-inch external drive bays, which can be filled with peripherals that need to be reached from the outside of the computer, such as CD-ROM drives, tape drives, card readers, front-mounted USB (universal serial bus) ports, and so on. Chassis may also have external 3½-inch drive bays for floppy drives and other small drives such as Zip drives and some tape drives. All chassis will include a number of internal 3½-inch bays, unreachable from the outside of the case, for mounting hard drives. Figure 1-2 shows the interior of a typical mid-tower case.

Figure 1-2
The interior of a typical mid-tower ATX case

As a general rule of thumb, a case with more expansion bays is better than a case with fewer expansion bays. You may be happy with your computer exactly the way it is, but at some point you might see a great deal on, say, a DVD-RAM drive and decide to buy it, and you'll need an external 5¼-inch bay for it. In addition, if you decide to add a hard drive, you'll need an interior 3½-inch bay for it.

Another factor in the expansion arena is the ease of adding a new gadget. Some cases let you slide 5¼-inch devices right through their front bezel and secure them with screws, while others require that you add special drive rails to facilitate mounting the device. Drive rails are an unnecessary and annoying extra step in the process.

Accessing the screw holes is another matter. Most cases allow you to slide their covers off and give you reasonable access to the screw holes necessary to secure drives in their housings and expansion cards in their slots. Find out whether a case makes it easy to reach the screw holes and whether the front bezel comes off easily, if necessary, to secure the smaller 3½-inch drives.

Speaking of 3½-inch drives, they can be even more difficult to wrangle into place than 5¼-inch drives. They tend to be tucked in to the front middle of mid-tower cases. Often, and most conveniently, they come in a form of a block that can be removed entirely from the PC, as shown in Figure 1-3. This lets you tinker with them on your table or workbench without having to jam your fingers into a mess of cabling and cramped space, and it prevents you from having to remove expansion cards (such as your video card) to install a hard drive, floppy drive, SuperDisk (LS120) drive, or whatever you plan to plant in the case.

Figure 1-3
The 3½-inch drive bay mount is removable in this case.

Other Considerations

If all that's not enough to think about in terms of a case, here are even more considerations. The size, the ease of disassembly, the options of front USB and other ports, and other factors can be important depending on your preferences.

Ease of disassembly—or how easily a case cover comes off and a case comes apart—is a paramount concern of hands-on PC enthusiasts. Tool-free cases have covers that come off without the use of tools, while traditional chassis require two or more screws (and a screwdriver) to secure the cover. In addition, some covers wrap completely around the case to cover both sides, while others are modular, with panels that cover the left and right sides separately.

Mounting a motherboard in a case is one of the most important parts of PC assembly. Some chassis make it easier than others. Many cases have removable motherboard mounting plates that let you mount and service a motherboard without having to dig through the inevitable snake's nest of ribbon and power cables when you have to work inside the case. Removable motherboard plates are a godsend for processor or CPU cooler upgrades.

As with all PC parts, the case plays a roll in the heat conductivity of the PC. We'll discuss cooling in depth in Chapter 5, but for now all you need to know is that the cooler it stays inside your PC, the better it is for your components. That's why aluminum cases are becoming increasingly popular. Aluminum conducts heat better than steel and allows the heat from the inside of the PC to dissipate throughout the case itself and mingle with the cooler outside air.

The size of your case is another consideration. Before buying a new case, you should measure the area in which you plan to put it and make sure there's enough room for the case you select. You may have big modding plans for a full-tower server case, only to discover that only a mid tower will fit into the available space. Most case manufacturers list the dimensions of their inventories on their web sites.

As a matter of convenience, some case manufactures have started offering front-mounted USBs and sometimes even FireWire ports. Similarly, some motherboards have auxiliary USB connectors that can be connected to these front-mounted ports. Since it's a pain to struggle around to the rear of a large case to plug in a USB peripheral, and because USB hubs cost money that you may not have to spend, front-mounted USB ports are a blessing. Be aware that not all motherboards will work with front-mounted USB and other ports.

Finally, ventilation is a factor. A good case will have a lot of fan mounts for 80mm fans and possibly a large mount for a 90mm or larger fan. It will also have lots of ambient ventilation holes to let air flow in or out of the system, depending upon whether you have a *negative* or *positive airflow system* (see Chapter 5).

Beware of Dell Power Supplies

Until the year 2000, Dell used proprietary power supplies and motherboards that looked a lot like ATX equipment. However, if you try to install a new motherboard with a Dell power supply, you risk damaging the motherboard. The only way to upgrade one of these Dells is to buy and insert both a motherboard and a power supply at the same time.

With or Without a Power Supply?

Many cases come with power supplies already mounted. This may sound like a bargain as well as a convenience, but as you'll see a little later in this chapter, you must take vast considerations into account when choosing a power supply. It's not necessarily a good idea to let a case manufacturer make that choice for you.

As mentioned, cases and power supplies are often overlooked components of computers. Between the two, the power supply is the more overlooked, making it the most underappreciated piece of equipment in an entire PC. That's a crime, since it's so vitally important to the operation of the PC itself.

I tend to choose cases without power supplies so that I can purchase a power supply to meet my system's individual needs. It's probably a good bet for you to do the same, since you're constructing a high-end, custom machine whose needs might not be fulfilled by a possibly generic and low-end power supply included with a case.

Some Favorite Cases

You should now be armed with enough information to choose a chassis for your computer. Since the last three chapters of this book, written by my distinguished co-author, Ed Chen, deal with modding, I'd like to add Ed's favorite modding cases:

❏ For a mid-tower system, the Enlight 7237

❏ For a full-tower system, the Chieftec Dragon steel and aluminum series

Both cases have lots of room to work with, and come with conveniences such as rounded edges and screwless drive mounts.

The Power Supply

Without a power supply, your computer would be nothing more than a doorstop. The power supply serves many purposes, from transforming the AC power fed into it into clean DC power for the PC's components to providing the proper current to each bit of equipment in the computer. Everything—the processor, the expansion bus, the BIOS, the motherboard chipset, the video and audio cards, the USB ports—rely on the proper operation of the power supply.

That makes it a vital component of the computer and one not to be overlooked or taken for granted. The following sections explain the anatomy of a power supply, how power supplies are used, and how to select the right power supply for your computer (overkill is a good thing). They explain the difference between a good, high-quality power supply and a cheapie knock-off that you'll want to avoid. They also explain how to mount a power supply into your chassis.

Suffice it to say, it's worth it to spend a little more time and money selecting the best power supply possible. (Note that a power supply is often referred to as a PSU, for power supply unit.)

What a Power Supply Does

To the typical user, the power supply's role is this: you plug your PC into the wall through it, flip the little switch (if there is one) to the "on" position, and then turn on the computer. From that moment, the power supply is forgotten, unless it has a really noisy fan—in which case, the user turns up the speakers.

Despite its seemingly simple roll in this scenario, the power supply is doing far more than it would seem. It's regulating current, transforming electricity from noisy AC to smooth DC, helping cool the system, and maybe even protecting the computer from damage caused by surges and brownouts.

The power supply furnishes the computer with the following voltages and devices powered:

Voltage	Devices Powered
+3.3V	Motherboard chipset, PCI and AGP cards, memory, serial and parallel ports
+5V	Voltage regulators, disk-drive controllers, legacy items like ISA slots and SIMM memory, PCI and AGP cards, serial and parallel ports
+12V	Motors, voltage regulators
–5V	Legacy ISA slots
–12V	Legacy serial and parallel ports

Since you'll probably be working with current ATX equipment, you can pretty much ignore the negative voltages. Figure 1-4 shows an ATX power supply.

Figure 1-4
An ATX
power supply

You can also ignore other legacies of older form factors, such as hot-toggle switches. An ATX power button doesn't do anything other than complete a logic circuit that tells the power supply to power up the system. Older form factors, such as AT, used actual switches in the front of the box that opened and closed an electrical circuit. Those switches had to be wired with a cable that stretched from the power supply to the front of the computer.

Current ATX power supplies (like the one shown in Figure 1-5) provide PS_ON (power on) and SVSB (SV Standby) current on a constant basis, unless they're shut off via the switch on the back or they are unplugged completely. This allows the PC to detect when the power-on circuit has been activated, and it also makes possible other functions, such as Wake on LAN, which allows remote programs on a network to wake the computer. This is often used by backup servers, maintenance programs implemented by a server, and other office stuff.

Figure 1-5
The rear of an
ATX power supply

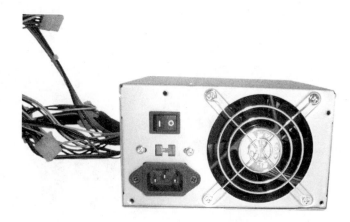

Along with supplying power to run a system, the power supply's job is to ensure that it's providing good, clean, DC current that's free of spikes, dips, and noise. It also makes sure that enough juice is provided to run the system. That's what the Power_Good signal is for. Most power supplies complete a series of internal checks and tests before powering up the system. If everything checks out, the power supply sends a signal to the motherboard called PWR_OK, or Power_Good, and that signal must be maintained continuously while the computer is on. If, for some reason, the normally 5V Power_Good signal fell outside its parameters (usually 2.5V to 6V), the power supply would cease to send the signal and the motherboard would reset the processor. Conditions that can cause the Power_Good signal to fail include brownouts, blackouts, and surges. Thus, the Power_Good signal is one way for the power supply to protect the PC from outside harm.

Beware that some low-priced, low-quality power supplies do not perform the necessary checks to maintain a proper Power_Good signal and instead simply send a 5V current through the circuit, thus ensuring that the motherboard thinks it's within normal parameters. That's one reason you shouldn't skimp on your purchase of a power supply.

Anatomy of an ATX Power Supply

Before you're ready to select a power supply, it might help you to understand exactly what goes into one. Figure 1-6 shows a naked power supply. A typical ATX power supply contains an integrated circuit board with the necessary capacitors, resistors, coils, and other electrical components needed to perform its duties. There's no need to go into detail here for two reasons: one, the power supply's printed circuit board (PCB) isn't considered a serviceable part, so if you blow a power supply or if it otherwise becomes damaged, it's best to replace it rather than tinker with its electronic innards; and two, it would take pages upon pages of explanation that would be better suited for an Electrical Engineering 101 textbook.

Figure 1-6
An ATX power
supply sans cover

Some power supplies may contain an on/off switch that can be used to kill the PS_ON, along with other small, ambient currents the power supply maintains when the computer is off. It contains a female power receptacle for a standard PC power cord. On the inside of the computer, it contains a jumble of wires and connectors, each of which we'll look at individually, and each of which is labeled in Figure 1-7.

Figure 1-7
An ATX power
supply and its parts

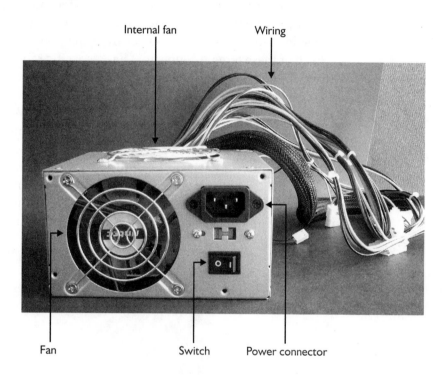

If you look at the rear (external) panel of the power supply (as shown in Figure 1-5), along with the possibility of an on/off switch, you'll see a female AC power connector, a fan blowhole for ventilation, and a switch to toggle between 115v and 230v input. In the United States, power is supplied at a level of 115v, but to make the power supply interchangeable so it can be used in Europe and elsewhere around the world, it also accepts the European standard of 230v.

Most computer power supplies are of a type called *switching* power supplies. These supplies not only try to put out constant DC voltage required by the PC no matter what kind of situation the incoming AC line is coughing up, but they also draw only the amount of current needed at a given time. This makes a switching power supply an efficient power source that uses a minimum of electricity.

ATX power supplies have two fans: a rear exhaust fan that blows air out of the back of the system, and an internal fan on the bottom of the power supply that blows air from the system into the power supply. This creates a *negative flow* cooling system (meaning that more air flows out of the system than into it, which creates a vacuum and draws air through the case's ambient holes).

Power Supply Connectors

Most ATX power supplies feature five types of connectors. They include connectors to provide power and auxiliary power to the motherboard, and power to the internal peripherals such as the hard drive, optical drives, and floppy drive. Even some video cards need power from the power supply.

Each of these female connectors has a specific range of pinouts, mostly consisting of +12V, +5V, and ground pins. Most were also designed by a company called Molex, and although Molex doesn't have a true monopoly on the power connectors within a PC, it's considerably dominant. We'll focus our attention on Molex connectors, since they're by far the most common. Figure 1-8 shows the primary power connector for an ATX motherboard. It's keyed in such a way that you can't connect it backward or otherwise erroneously. It provides plenty of 12V, 5V, and 3.3V lines, as well as the Power_Good connector and several ground wires. Athlon-based systems currently require only this connector to run everything on the motherboard, including the processor and all of the core logic.

Figure 1-8
The 20-pin main ATX motherboard power supply connector (Molex 39-01-2200)

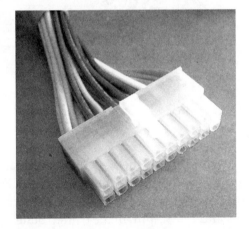

Included with standard version 2.03 specification power supplies, the 12V connector is used chiefly by modern Pentium 4 motherboards (see Figure 1-9). The voltage requirements of the processor exceed the voltage provided by the main 20-pin connector, and thus this connector, which consists of two 12V leads and two grounds, is used to allow the system to draw the extra current required. It's similarly keyed to prevent an incorrect connection.

Figure I-9
ATX 12V connector
(required for
some Pentium 4
motherboards)
(Molex 39-01-2040)

12V Connectors

Some motherboards bypass the 12V connector by providing standard sockets for Molex 15-24-4048 connectors. This is a boon for people with an older power supply lacking a 12V connector who wish to upgrade to a Pentium 4 motherboard and processor. If you buy your power supply new, however, make sure it has the extra 12V lead; chances are, it will.

When memory was changed to draw 3.3V, its draw to maintain sufficient amperage became greater. Although rarely used, the auxiliary connector shown in Figure 1-10 was added to the power supply specification of 250W or greater power supplies to supply the extra current. If your motherboard doesn't have a receptacle for this power connector, simply ignore it.

Figure I-I0
ATX auxiliary
power connector
(Molex 8993)

In the snake's nest of wires that billows out of the power supply, the peripheral power connector (Figure 1-11) is the most common connector that you'll find. The peripheral connectors are used to power most of the interior devices in the system. Even if you run short of peripheral connectors, you can use a Y-splitter (Figure 1-12), available at any good computer store, to add more connectors.

Figure 1-11
A peripheral
power connector
(Molex 15-24-4048)

Figure 1-12
A peripheral
connector Y-splitter

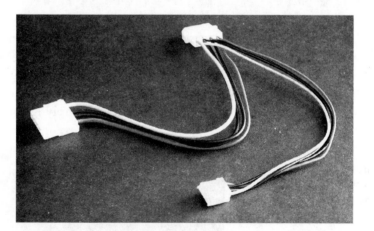

Smaller peripheral connectors (Figure 1-13) are far less common than the larger ones. Most power supplies have only one or two of these, and they're most commonly used for powering the floppy drive, although some other small drives such as SuperDisk (LS-120) drives also use them.

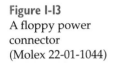

Figure 1-13
A floppy power
connector
(Molex 22-01-1044)

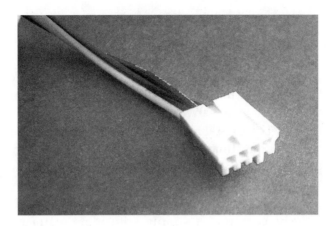

Choosing a Power Supply

Now that you understand the role and components of a power supply, it's time for you to decide on a power supply of your own. Of course, you need to consider a few factors when you're preparing to choose one. Remember that you'll want one that will last a long time, at least through several upgrades, and possibly for the entire life of your computer.

When choosing a power supply, treat your decision as seriously as you would when choosing any other aspect of your system. In the beginning of this chapter, you read that the power supply is one of the most overlooked and disregarded components of a PC—hopefully, you now know enough about this vital component to dispel that myth.

Here's what to consider when you choose a power supply.

Load

Power supplies are rated in *wattage* (W), which can be determined by multiplying voltage and amperage. This is a tedious way to figure load, but you can, if you wish, determine the current needs of every device and peripheral you plan to assemble in your PC and choose a power supply based on your calculations. For example, a motherboard might use 5A (amps) of power on a 5V line, requiring 25W. A floppy drive's logic uses .5A at 5V, for 2.5W. Two PCI slots filled use 4A, and this is all powered by the 5V current, so there's another 20 watts. Meanwhile, the 12V current powers the 3½-inch drive motor with 1A, the floppy motor also uses 1A, and CD and DVD-ROM drives use 1A each—chalk up 48 more watts.

You can crunch the numbers by using $V \times A$ and come up with a wattage requirement if you wish, and you can obtain the voltage and amperage requirements of every peripheral you plan to install. If you do this, buy a power supply with a greater capacity than you need to cover for any upgrades that you may add in the future. For example, if you end up calculating that you need 268W, get a 300W or 350W power supply.

There is a simpler way. Consider that you're going to be using your computer for a long time. You might add new drives at any time, you may upgrade the processor and/or motherboard, and you might add a hard drive. Since you're not building a disposable system, but one that you can upgrade as needed, your system is unlikely to be static for a long period of time. Therefore, you'll want to choose a power supply with more wattage than you currently need. For a high-end gamer's system like you're going to build, you shouldn't go with less than a 350W or 400W power supply.

TIPS OF THE TRADE

Power Supplies: Go Large

When selecting a power supply for a computer that you plan to use for a long time, overkill is good. Get something with more power than you think you'll ever need. Power supplies last a long time, and there's no good reason to have to upgrade one down the line when your power needs increase because you skimped when you bought your original. When in doubt, go for excess power.

Protection

Not all power supplies are equal in terms of how well they protect your system from brownouts, blackouts, and surges. High-end power supplies contain safety circuitry that will protect the other components in your system, even at the expense of the power supply itself.

Look for power supplies with PC protecting features that can deal with problematic AC. This is especially important if you don't use an external power protection device, such as a surge protector, a power conditioner, or a UPS, which are all discussed in their own sections a little later in the chapter.

Noise

Throughout this book, the noise factor of your PC is discussed. It's no fun to play games and work next to a computer that sounds like a Leer jet taking off for Maui. Power supplies are one of the noisiest components in the PC with their dual fans running all the time. Only recently have power supply manufacturers begun to address this issue, adding tricks like heat-sensitive fans that adjust their RPM speed according to the cooling needs, or just plain quiet-running fans.

Brands

You *don't* want a generic power supply. As with most components, it's always better to spend a little more money on a name-brand item. You'll get a better warranty, accessible tech support, and generally better quality than you will with a generic model. Some brands to look at for power supplies are Antec, PC Power and Cooling, and Enlight. My personal favorite power supply, which fulfills all of these conditions, is Antec's TruePower line, available in a number of watt ratings. I tend to go with the True430 for my high-end systems.

Your PSU and Your Motherboard

Make sure your power supply and your motherboard (covered in Chapter 2) are compatible. As noted earlier, AT and ATX motherboards have different connectors. We're focusing on ATX equipment, so be sure to get an ATX v.2.03-compliant power supply.

Power Protection

AC power is noisy, and it's prone to brownouts, surges, and other destructive factors that can damage a power supply or even internal computer components. No matter how wonderful your power supply is, it's a good idea to have some sort of external power protection to keep destructive AC influences from reaching your PC altogether.

External power protection comes in a bunch of different forms and at all kinds of price points. Surge protectors are usually inexpensive, line conditioners are priced in the middle, and uninterruptible power supplies (UPSs) are relatively expensive. Each offers a different level of protection.

Surge Protectors

Surge protectors, or suppressors, can clip surges, sending excess power to ground, but they're useless against brownouts. They generally use devices called *metal oxide varistors (MOVs)*, which can accept a certain amount of power while shunting excess current. MOVs can gradually degrade, however, through a series of small surges, and they can be blown useless by a major spike such as a lightning strike. Often, it's difficult to tell when a surge suppressor has become useless due to a worn MOV unless it has a light to indicate the status of the MOV. Look for this if you buy a surge suppressor, and make sure it's compliant to the UL 1449 standard, a high-quality standard that ensures good, solid protection.

Power Conditioners

Available for $200 to $300, a power or line conditioner does the job of a surge protector and more. It contains a complex range of circuitry and acts as an active device, constantly monitoring the status of an AC line. It's able to supply power to make up for the loss during a temporary brownout, clip the worst of surges, and generally keep a clean stream of AC current running to your computer. It's an excellent device to own if your PC shares a line with something that causes occasional dips in power when it starts up, such as a washing machine, a dishwasher, or a furnace. Note that line conditioners can't prevent your system from going down in the case of a blackout.

Uninterruptible Power Supplies

For the ultimate in power protection, a battery backup is paramount. UPS devices contain just that. Able to condition a line as well as any line conditioner, a UPS, available for anywhere from $200 to thousands of dollars depending on the size of the battery and other factors, adds the security of keeping the computer working for a limited period of time even in the event of a total blackout. Note that UPSs are not intended to run the computer for more than a few minutes—they're intended to keep it on for just enough time to shut down the system gracefully. Intelligent UPSs can interface with the operating system and do this automatically.

Many distinguishing factors separate one UPS from another, including the amount of backup time they provide and the amount of power they consume. When a blackout occurs, a UPS's battery will gradually discharge as it powers the computer connected to it; when power returns, it will automatically recharge its battery. A UPS is the ultimate device in power protection. A powerful surge, such as a close lightning strike, can still damage your PC no matter how well it's protected.

Installing a Power Supply

When you've finally made all the important decisions about powering your computer, including choosing a power supply and the use of external power protection, it's time to install the power supply into the chassis. If you're starting from scratch in the creation of your new super system, you've probably got a bare, empty chassis with lots of holes in it and not much else to speak of.

Securing the PSU

The first thing you'll need to do is figure out how to get the cover off your case. If you purchased a tool-free chassis, look for a latch or other release. Otherwise, you'll probably need a medium-sized Philips head screwdriver to remove the case cover.

Chassis covers can be modular, meaning that various sides come off independently. Often the entire cover comes off in one fell swoop (except for the front bezel, which almost always comes off by itself). Determine which type you're working with by checking for seams at the corners of the case cover.

The power supply itself is held in place by four screws that come through the rear of the case. Getting the power supply into place can be tricky, depending on the makeup of the chassis. The power supply should be situated so that the larger fan (on its bottom) faces down into the case, while the panel with the smaller fan and the AC connector faces out the back of the machine, as shown in Figure 1-14.

Figure 1-14
Situating a
power supply

Have four wide-thread screws ready. Wrangle the PSU into place, being wary of hazards such as guide panels, support pillars, and so on.

TIPS OF THE TRADE

Securing the PSU

Insert one screw and screw it in partway, and then deal with the remaining three screws. When each screw is partially tightened and the power supply is in place, tighten each screw completely.

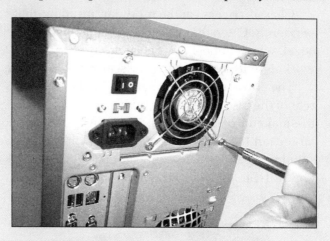

Reigning in the Wires

Inside the case, you'll see a jumble of wires. Make sure they make their way down into the chassis. If a support beam appears across the side of the case, run the wires through the opening behind it. For now, before you've inserted the motherboard and peripherals, you can stuff the wires into the 5¼-inch drive bays. This will make it easier to install the motherboard, assuming your case doesn't have a removable motherboard panel. If it does, don't worry about where the power supply cables lie just yet.

Later, when you've got most of the system assembled, you'll want to get the cables under control. You might want to secure them to available metal struts with cable ties, which will move them out of the way and foster good airflow through the case. But that's for the future; as long as you've gotten the power supply secure, you're finished with this chapter.

That Was the Easy Part

You've got power in your case, but right now there's nothing to use it on. We'll get into connecting the motherboard and other peripherals in later chapters. Now that your computer has skin and a beating heart, it's time to give it a brain. That comes in the form of a CPU, or central processing unit, which is discussed in detail in the next chapter.

Chapter 2

The Motherboard, Processor, and Memory

Tools of the Trade

A pair of pliers
A medium Philips head screwdriver

Now that you've picked out a case, you need something to put in it. The core of your system will consist of three parts: the motherboard, which houses such important items as the BIOS, processor socket, memory slots, and buses that provide pathways for data; the central processor, which does most of the actual computing and radically affects the overall performance of the system; and the memory, where data is stored for processing by the various processors in the machine.

Your choice of any one of these components directly affects the other three, because the three work in unison and determine each other's compatible specifications. AMD Athlon processors, for example, require a specific type of motherboard that's incompatible with Intel Pentium processors, and some motherboards work with Double Data Rate (DDR) memory while others work with Rambus RAM. Once you've decided on, purchased, and installed the motherboard, central processing unit (CPU), and memory triplets, you'll have the core of a killer gaming rig. Combined with the graphics card (which is covered in the next chapter), these components determine how fast and efficiently your computer will run games and other applications.

This chapter discusses only the latest and fastest hardware available. To use less would mean that you'd have to upgrade sooner, so the system parts recommended here should help you keep up with the latest graphics-heavy games for at least a couple of years.

The Motherboard

The motherboard is the system's spine—an important part of the central nervous system that carries data to and from the rest of the system. Because its roll is so vital, it's important that you choose a high-quality board.

Some would even argue that the motherboard is the single most important part that goes into a PC, and for good reason. Your choice of a motherboard determines which processors you can add to your system and what kind of memory is compatible with your PC. Its houses PCI (Peripheral Component Interface) expansion slots, so it determines how many cards can be inserted into your system. It also houses the Accelerated Graphics Port (AGP) slot and controller, so it determines the AGP *bandwidth* (the conduit between the main memory bank and the graphics card).

Your motherboard's *form factor* (the size, shape, and other physical and electrical attributes) must match the case you've chosen. Since we've focused on ATX cases so far, the first thing you'll need to know about your choice of motherboard is that it needs to be an ATX model. That's not a limiting factor, because the vast majority of motherboards manufactured *are* ATX boards. After reading a brief discussion about the function of the motherboard, you'll learn how to choose one and install it in your system.

Buses, Slots, and Controllers

The motherboard (Figure 2-1) is the ultimate telephone system. It lets all of the components of the PC, including the processor, memory, expansion cards, and all the controllers housed on the board itself, talk to each other at unimaginable speeds.

It does this through the use of *buses*, which are wires that carry data around the board:

❏ The *AGP* bus, which gives an AGP graphics card direct access to the system memory. It can store textures in main memory that it doesn't have room for in its own local memory.

❏ The *PCI* bus, which carries data to and from expansion cards, such as sound cards, network interface cards (NICs), modems, and other PCI cards.

❏ The *front-side* bus (FSB), which carries data to and from the system's CPU.

Figure 2-1
A typical
motherboard

Each bus works at its own speed set by its *controller*, a logic chip that maintains the flow of traffic through its bus. The PCI bus operates at 33MHz on nearly every motherboard available today. The other two buses vary according to the motherboard you purchase.

The speed of the AGP bus is referred to in multiples of the original AGP specification. Currently, motherboards and graphics cards support both 4X and 8X AGP, but you'll want to go with the latter. 4X AGP transfers data at 1066 megabytes per second, and 8X AGP cranks up its engines at 2100 megabytes per second (or 2.1 gigabytes per second). 8X AGP is just emerging at the time of this writing, but some benchmarks already show that it improves gaming performance in texture-heavy games such as *Unreal Tournament 2003*.

The FSB affects data headed to or returning from the CPU, which, of course, is the heart of the system. Current FSBs run at 400MHz or 533MHz for Intel Pentium–based computers, and 333MHz for AMD Athlon XP PCs.

Buses aren't the only components dependent on the motherboard. Your choice of a motherboard will also determine your system's expansion limits, its data transfer speed to the hard drive, and the range of special features offered by the board.

The motherboard houses both PCI and memory slots. The number of PCI slots it offers can be crucial if you purchase a number of upgrade cards. While most systems contain only a sound card and a network adapter or modem, there's no telling what you may want in the future. You may decide to purchase a Small Computer System Interface (SCSI) adapter that would occupy another slot, a hardware MPEG (Moving Pictures Expert Group) decoder that would fill yet another vacancy, and so on. As a general rule of thumb, more expansion slots are better.

The AGP Slot Stands Alone

Don't look for a motherboard with multiple AGP slots, even if you want a second display adapter. They do not exist. However, if you need multiple displays, most current video cards offer dual-display support.

It's also nice to have free memory slots when you decide to upgrade your system's RAM. You can do two things to ensure that you don't have to pull a module to insert a larger one. (When you're reduced to doing that, you'll end up with a perfectly good memory stick sitting on a shelf.) First, buy one large module to start with when you first build your PC. Second, buy a motherboard with plenty of memory slots.

Various motherboards offer wide ranges of features. Some have onboard audio solutions—but don't be concerned with them because they pale in comparison to high-end sound cards.

Stuff that you might want includes the following:

❏ **A serial ATA controller**   This interfaces with fast serial ATA hard drives. (Storage is discussed in Chapter 5.)

❏ **USB 2.0 ports**   USB 2.0 is much faster than its predecessor, USB 1.1. Devices such as external CD-RW (CD-rewritable) burners are already available for the new USB standard.

❏ **FireWire ports**   These ports are especially useful if you're into digital video editing. Most digital camcorders interface with FireWire, allowing for speedy transfer of video to and from your PC.

❏ **IDE RAID**   RAID (for Redundant Array of Independent Disks) offers two advantages: speed and security.

❏ **Other features**   Card readers, integrated Ethernet, and the capability to tweak and overclock the board.

AMD, Intel, and That Other One

Your choice of motherboard directly affects the processor that you can use in your system. Motherboard architecture is built around specific processor families, so you can't use, say, an Athlon processor in a Pentium 4 motherboard.

Two major players and one dark horse dominate the processor market. Intel, the king of processor sales since the dawn of personal computers, has its Pentium line squared off against AMD's Athlon processors, which are less expensive than

Pentiums and just as powerful. The third brand, Cyrix, is owned by VIA, and while it was a growing force in CPUs a few years ago, it's since taken a back seat to Intel and AMD.

Cyrix processors aren't positioned to compete against Intel and AMD wares. They're designed around small footprint, budget-priced PCs, and they don't have the horsepower for high-performance gaming.

One aspect that differentiates the various motherboards is their *processor sockets*. AMD Athlon XP motherboards feature Socket A, a receptacle for Athlon and Athlon XP processors with 462 pins. Current Intel motherboards feature a smaller socket, but one with more pinholes—478 to be exact. That's not the only difference between the two. The core architectures of the motherboards differ to make them compatible with their CPUs. Athlon processors support an FSB clocked at 333MHz, while newer Pentium 4 CPUs support FSBs running as high as 533MHz. Furthermore, Athlon CPUs support DDR memory, while Intel supports DDR or Rambus modules, depending on the motherboard.

In real-world performance, both AMD and Intel offer cutting-edge solutions. The latest processors at the time of this writing—the Athlon XP 2800+ and the Pentium 4 3.06GHz—are both ultra-high-performance parts. The Pentium 4, paired with Rambus memory, edges out the Athlon, but it does so by a narrow margin and it costs a lot more.

Chipsets

The defining factor of a motherboard is its *chipset*. Intel and AMD each make their own chipsets, and VIA Technologies is a popular third-party chipset manufacturer that makes chipsets for both the Pentium 4 and Athlon XP processor families. Other, less widespread, chipsets are manufactured by SiS and Acer Labs.

A chipset consists mainly of two chips seated on the motherboard. The *northbridge* defines the type of CPU and memory with which the board will be compatible, the AGP specification, and the speed of the FSB. The *southbridge* handles other functions including interfacing with the serial, parallel, and USB controllers; the onboard audio and Ethernet chips; the PCI bus; the IDE channels; and other components.

Intel offers a wide range of chipsets in its 845 and 850 families. The former uses DDR memory, which is more affordable but not quite as fast as the Rambus memory used by the latter. AMD is less aggressive in its chipset manufacturing, making only the 760 chipset for its Athlon XP processors.

VIA, SiS, and Acer chipsets tend to be closer to the cutting edge than the more conservative chipsets from the processor manufacturers. Their products were the first to feature AGP 8X support, for example.

Choosing a Motherboard

Choosing a motherboard is more difficult than buying a car. The market is overwhelming, with more than a dozen major manufacturers, each usually with several current motherboards in circulation at any given time.

First, you'll need to decide which processor family you wish to go with. The vast majority of solutions use DDR memory; it's getting hard to find Rambus motherboards for current processors. For bleeding-edge performance at any cost, the Pentium 4 3.06GHz with PC3200 (400MHz DDR) is king. For a more cost-effective but still extremely fast solution, look at an Athlon XP 2800+ with PC3200 memory.

Next, you'll have to decide on a motherboard brand. This author has tested and benchmarked hundreds of motherboards through the years. The best brands consistently have been SOYO, ASUS, ABIT, and DFI. If you're building your first system and you've never handled a new motherboard, add Gigabyte to the list; its boards come with the friendliest documentation and installation guides available.

Specific motherboards recommendations, based on performance and features, are listed in the following table:

Pentium 4	Athlon XP
SOYO P4X400 DRAGON Ultra Platinum Edition (supports processors up to 2.8GHz only)	SOYO KT400 DRAGON Ultra Platinum Edition
DFI NB80-EA	ABIT KD7-G
ASUS P4PE	ASUS A7V8X

Choosing between Intel and AMD is difficult. We recommend AMD, mainly because its parts are cheaper than Intel's, it runs equally well, and AMD-based computers tend to be more upgradeable than Intel-based systems. Intel often creates new motherboard architectures, forcing frequent upgraders to buy not only a new CPU but a new motherboard as well.

Our current favorite motherboard is the SOYO KT400 Dragon Ultra, in its shiny and showy Platinum Edition. The edition describes the color of the board, and this one comes in a nifty silver color. A black edition is also available.

Installing the Motherboard

When you've chosen a motherboard, it's time to roll up your sleeves and get busy. Be sure you know how to open the case, and if your case's motherboard panel comes out, know how to remove it and replace it. You might also want to

Important Info About ESD

ESD, Electrostatic Discharge, is what happens when you rub your feet on a carpet and then touch someone else. That little burst of static electricity that stings your finger is more than enough of a charge to damage a delicate chip permanently on a piece of computer equipment. Most components are shipped in anti-static bags, which are usually silver in color.

It's very important to be static-safe when you're handling the insides of your computer. Try not to work in a carpeted area, and follow these steps to handle your equipment safely and thwart ESD:

1. Before removing a component from an anti-static bag or touching anything inside your PC, plant your feet and ground yourself by touching something metal.

2. Keep your feet planted, and handle the component by the edges whenever it's possible. Expansion cards may be held by the metal gate that faces the rear of the computer.

3. If you move your feet, plant them and ground yourself again.

4. When you're not using a component, keep it in an anti-static bag.

Another option is to purchase an anti-static bracelet, which you wear on one wrist and connect via a wire to a ground, such as your computer case. The bracelet maintains contact between you and the ground, preventing you from building up a charge. Anti-static bracelets are available at most computer shops and online from such merchants as Buy.com and ULINE (www.uline.com).

remove the 3-inch drive bay bracket if it comes out, as it does on most tower and mid-tower cases.

1. Take the cover off your case, or open the cover if it has individual panels. Take off the panel that, with the case's front bezel facing you, is on the left side. Lay the case on its side with the open side facing up and the front bezel facing you.

2. If your case's motherboard mounting panel comes out, remove it and work on it instead of working through the case.

3. Your case should have come with mounting hardware in a bag or box somewhere inside. Find it, open it up, and separate out the brass

standoffs (the little brass double-threaded risers that support the motherboard).

4. Find the screw holes in the motherboard. Each of those holes corresponds to a hole in the metal panel that houses the motherboard. Insert a standoff in each corresponding hole, and tighten each one with a pair of pliers.

5. Your motherboard may have come with a small, rectangular panel with holes of various shapes and sizes cut out of it. Look for it. That's the bezel for the I/O port riser, and it needs to go in the back of the case near the power supply. Carefully remove the bezel that came with the motherboard, and insert the new one, snapping it into place. If your motherboard did not come with an I/O port riser bezel, don't worry about it.

6. Next, insert the motherboard into the case, wriggling it carefully past any drive bays that are in the way, until it lays flat on the grid of standoffs. Then slide the motherboard toward the back of the case so that the I/O ports fit snugly against the bezel. Some of the ports, like the serial and parallel ports, will actually go through the bezel.

7. The motherboard screw holes should be close to being lined up with the brass standoffs. Finish lining them up and continue on.

Two Types of Screws

Two styles of mounting screws are associated with PCs—one with narrow threads and another with wider threads. Usually, the standoffs accept screws with the narrower thread, but there's no set standard. The best way to find out which screws your risers work with is to try inserting a large screw; if it doesn't turn easily, insert a narrow screw and try turning it.

8. Insert a screw through the motherboard into one of the standoffs. Turn it a couple of times, but don't tighten it entirely. Add screws to each of the other holes, turning each one a few times but not tightening them. When you've finished inserting all of the screws, go back around and tighten them snugly. Don't over-tighten them or you can crack the motherboard.

9. With your motherboard firmly in place, it's time to connect the power supply to it. Find the largest plug, and match it to the white receptacle on the motherboard. It will go in only one way, so you can't connect it

backward. Insert it until it's snug. If you're using a Pentium 4 motherboard with the proper power supply, you'll see a separate, four-wire power lead that you have to connect.

When you're finished, you're motherboard is in place and ready for action.

The Processor

Continuing with the biological metaphor, the brain of your PC is the main processor, or CPU. Although other processors are included in the system for video acceleration, audio-digital signal processing, and other processes, the CPU does the vast majority of the grunt work, crunching calculations with enormous speed and efficiency.

In fact, the power of the CPU is often considered to be the main identifying factor in a computer. When someone is asked what type of system she has, her first words describe the processor ("I have a Pentium 4, 1500 megahertz…"). Indeed, for a hardcore gaming machine, the processor and the motherboard on which it resides are the most important components, with the memory and graphics card both close behind.

The CPU is the pivotal unit that executes the vast majority of calculations in the computer. In games, it processes important things like artificial intelligence, weapons and damage calculations, and other goings on. With older 3-D graphics cards, the CPU processes part of the graphics pipeline. (See Chapter 4.)

Motherboards, the main circuit boards of computers, are built around processors. As faster processors are released, or as processors' form factors change, new motherboards are built to accommodate them.

For years, Intel has dominated the processor market. The first PCs, manufactured by IBM in 1981, contained a 4.77MHz Intel processor called the 8088. It wasn't the first computer system, but it effectively defined personal computing for a long tine to come.

CPUs have come a long way since then. Nowadays, PC processors run at more than 3000MHz, and many other improvements have been made. IBM is no longer the only company building PCs, but all PCs are called "IBM compatible" or "clones" because with the original PC, IBM defined the standards that are still in effect today.

What the Processor Does

The processor performs most of the major calculations that trickle through your PC. The processor thinks in 0's or 1's (bits) and uses a vast number of transistors to receive, store, and return data. To give you an idea of the vastness of a processor's internal capacity, an Athlon XP has more than 37 million transistors within its tiny core. The CPUs we're concentrating on run the x86 instruction set. They also have enhancements, such as MMX (Multimedia Extensions), SSE (Streaming SIMD (Single Instruction, Multiple Data) Extensions), and 3DNow!, which are special instruction sets that programmers use to enhance their software and make it run more quickly and smoothly on a PC.

The CPU is often defined by the speed at which it operates. It can also be identified by its width and other important factors that are often ignored. We'll start by explaining exactly what processor "speed" is.

Frequency

CPUs are measured in speed—or, to be more accurate, frequency, in megahertz or gigahertz. One hertz is one cycle per second. Were you to, say, tap your knee once every second, your knee-tapping frequency would be one hertz. One megahertz is one *million* cycles per second, and a gigahertz is one *billion* cycles per second. You probably can't tap your knee that fast, at least not without some serious bruising, but current processors run at speeds well over one gigahertz.

Speed is tied closely to the price of the processor. Usually, when a higher speed processor is released to market, lower speed processors drop in price. Sometimes you can get a real bargain by getting a processor that's been available for a few months and surpassed in speed, rather than demanding the absolute cutting edge. However, keep in mind that the processor speed makes the biggest difference in overall system performance.

The frequency rating indicates the core clock speed of the processor, and it affects only calculations that are going on inside the processor. The size of the internal *registers* determine how much information the processor can work on at the same time. Most current processors have 32-bit registers. That means they're capable of dealing with 32-bit wads of data, whereas a 16-bit processor, like the 286, can not.

Pentium-class processors use a 64-bit *data I/O bus*. This is the processor's external data bus that shovels data into and out of the processor. Pentium introduced *superscalar architecture,* which means it has two 32-bit *pipelines* in which to process data. The dual pipelines, at 32 bits each, match perfectly with the 64-bit data I/O bus.

Yet another bus, the *address bus*, is used to describe to the processor the memory locations of the data it needs to receive. Current generation processors use 36-bit address buses, also referred to as 36 *address lines*.

All of these processor buses are described by their width in bits. The wider the bus, the better. Think of it this way: a single 1-inch garden hose can carry a certain amount of water. If you add another 1-inch hose, they can carry twice as much water as a 1-inch hose by itself can. Use two more hoses, and you've doubled the water capacity again. The more hoses you add, the more water you can siphon at the same time.

Note that the data bus, the register size, and the address bus, while all vitally important, don't directly affect the core frequency of the processor. A faster processor will always outmode a slower one.

Megahertz and Athlon Product Marking

Until recently, all processors were sold with a rating in megahertz or gigahertz. For example, Pentium 4s come in 2.4GHz, 2.53GHz, 2.8GHz, 3.06GHz, and so on. AMD's Athlons, however, are no longer marked with their true clock frequencies. Instead, AMD has adopted a marking scheme that supposedly describes the Pentium-equivalent speed. This description is called a *P-rating*.

For example, an Athlon XP 1500+ actually runs at 1333MHz, but according to AMD it compares in performance to a Pentium 4 1500MHz. Whether this is actually the case is the subject of heated debate in the hardware community; some benchmarks back up AMD's theory and some don't. For comparison, check out the Athlon P-ratings and actual megahertz speeds in Table 2-1.

Note that Table 2-1 indicates the speeds of processors based on AMD's current Thoroughbred core. The latest Athlons, from the 2700+ and upward, support a 333MHz FSB, while earlier ones support a 266MHz core. All support 333MHz and 400MHz DDR memory.

Athlon XP P-Rating	Actual Speed in MHz
1700+	1467
1800+	1533
1900+	1600
2000+	1667
2100+	1733
2200+	1800
2400+	2000
2600+	2130
2700+	2170
2800+	2250

Table 2-1
Athlon XP P-Ratings and Actual Clock Speeds

Cooling

As processors have become more sophisticated, they've grown in the sheer number of transistors they incorporate. More transistors means more current is passing through them, and more heat is generated. Today's processors require *active* coolers (heat sinks with fans attached). Earlier processors used *passive* coolers (heat sinks without fans), and even earlier ones didn't require cooling at all.

If you run a current processor without a cooler, it'll fry itself permanently in a matter of seconds. With the number of transistors in processors skyrocketing, cooling is becoming more and more important to processor health.

One thing in our favor that helps keep processors from melting down is the continually shrinking die processes used by chip makers. The *process* indicates the spacing and the size of the components on a chip. To give you an example of how quickly chips are shrinking, consider that in 1990 most processors were made on a 1-micron die. Current Pentium 4s are made on a 0.13-micron die! The smaller the process a processor is built on, the less heat it generates.

So the heat battle is balanced: as the die shrinks, the more transistors are crammed into a chip. More transistors make a hotter chip; smaller processes run cooler.

No matter what, you'll need an active heat sink on your processor. If you buy it in a retail kit, rather than a "white box," you might get an appropriate cooler right in the package. However, if you go the cheaper route of getting an original equipment manufacturer (OEM) processor, you'll need to buy your own cooler.

Currently, Athlons and Pentium 4s require different coolers. Athlon coolers fasten to little hooks right on the socket, while Pentium 4 coolers fasten to the motherboard via a housing that surrounds the socket.

Your cooler will consist of a large heat sink—a metal block, usually aluminum or copper or a mix thereof, with fins or pillars designed to dissipate heat from whatever it's attached to. It will include a fan attached to the heat sink, to help speed the heat dissipation. It'll also come with mounting hardware. Most coolers come with a strip of thermal tape or a small amount of thermal paste, which is necessary to ensure good contact between the cooler and the CPU, as each may have imperfections on its surfaces that, on a microscopic level, keeps it from being perfectly flat. Figure 2-2 shows an example of a CPU cooler.

Coolers can be purchased at most computer stores and at cooling-dedicated sites such as *www.frozencpu.com* and *www.coolerguys.com*. Brands such as Thermaltake and Alpha make excellent active coolers, and some of their wares come with nifty-colored LEDs. Make sure you get a cooler rated for the clock frequency of your CPU.

Figure 2-2
A Thermaltake
Volcano 7 CPU cooler

You may also need thermal paste if it doesn't come with the unit. Some coolers come with thermal tape fixed to the area of the heat sink that will make contact with the processor. If yours doesn't, you'll need thermal compound (shown in Figure 2-3), such as Arctic Silver III, which is available at the web sites just mentioned. Thermal compound or tape is necessary to foster good contact between the heat sink and the CPU, which in turn ensures that the cooler will whisk heat away from the CPU.

HEADS UP!

Coolers Are Not Optional

Without proper cooling, your CPU won't operate properly. It might even roast itself to death. A good cooler is not an option; it's a necessity. Never operate a PC without an active cooler affixed to the CPU, even for a few seconds. That's all the time it takes for a CPU to destroy itself.

Figure 2-3
A tube of thermal
compound

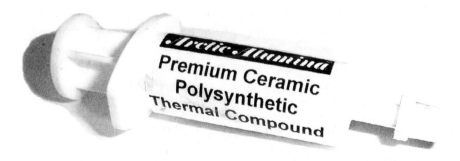

For the hardcore, there are alternatives to simple air/heat sink cooling. You can purchase water cooling kits, which run water from a reservoir through a radiator and then through a block attached to a processor. Some people even use Peltier elements, which are flat, electronic elements that aggressively pull heat from one side and dissipate it through the other. Such coolers are used mainly for overclocking the processor.

Choosing a CPU

If you've already chosen your motherboard, your choice of a CPU is a natch: get the fastest one you can afford that's compatible with your motherboard. Only one of our motherboard recommendations is limited to a certain speed, the SOYO P4X400 DRAGON Ultra, and that's because Pentium 4 processors larger than 3GHz require a new motherboard with support for Hyper-Threading Technology (a new CPU twist that allows the processor to run two threads, or parts of programs, simultaneously).

If you've been holding off choosing a motherboard until you chose your processor, consider these factors:

- ❏ Pentium processors are currently available at higher clock frequencies than Athlon CPUs. The latest Pentium 4 is mildly faster than the fastest Athlon XP.

- ❏ Pentiums undergo the best testing regimens in the industry, ensuring across-the-board compatibility.

- ❏ History has shown that it's easier to upgrade Athlon-based systems. Intel processors often require new motherboard technology.

- ❏ Athlon-based systems deliver a better price/performance ratio.

Because of the ease of upgrading and the friendlier prices, we recommend an AMD Athlon processor (see Figure 2-4). It's not an easy decision, however, as Pentium 4 CPUs at 3.06GHz outperform Athlon XP 2800+ CPUs, but only by a narrow margin. AMD processors are great because of their speed and easy upgradeability, but Pentium tends to offer new technologies faster than AMD. The following installation demonstration uses the Athlon XP 2800+. Note that if price is not a factor and you want the absolute highest performance available, a Pentium 4 is the answer.

Installing Your CPU and Cooler

It's a relatively simple process to install a CPU into a system, but nonetheless you need to be careful when handling the delicate parts. CPUs mount in sockets

Figure 2-4
An Athlon CPU

called *ZIF sockets* (for Zero Insertion Force). They feature handles that, when raised, open up the holes and allow you to drop the CPU into place without pressing on it. Let's get going.

1. Locate the CPU socket on your motherboard. After you're sure that you're static-safe, gently unsnap and raise the handle next to it. Figure 2-5 shows how it should look.

Figure 2-5
A socket with the handle open

2. Now look at the pin configuration on the underside of your CPU. If you're installing an Athlon XP, two of the corners will be lacking a few pins (Figure 2-6); if you're installing a Pentium 4, only one of the corners will be irregular.

3. Line up the oddball corners with the corresponding corners on the socket. Carefully lay the CPU down onto the ZIF socket and, if necessary, press it down with a minimum of force. It should drop into place without any force at all, but sometimes it needs a gentle push.

Don't Force It!

Never force a CPU into its socket. You can bend the pins and ruin the processor. If the CPU doesn't drop in with minimal pressure when the socket lever is up, make sure you've lined it up properly.

4. When the processor is seated, return the handle to its down position and snap it into place, as shown in Figure 2-7. That will seal the processor into the socket so that it can't be removed without lifting the handle again.

That's all there is to inserting the CPU; next you have to install the cooler. Pentium 4 coolers and Athlon XP coolers differ significantly.

Figure 2-6
Athlon XP CPU pins

Figure 2-7
Inserting an
Athlon CPU

Installing a Pentium 4 Cooler

Here's how you install a Pentium 4 cooler (shown in Figure 2-8).

1. Locate the black base bracket surrounding the CPU. Note the four tall
    pillars, one in each corner. The cooler's bracket will align with the
    motherboard bracket and snap into notches on the base. The cooler has
    two levers that, when set, apply pressure to the heat sink to keep it in
    solid contact with the CPU (Figure 2-9).

Figure 2-8
A Pentium 4 cooler

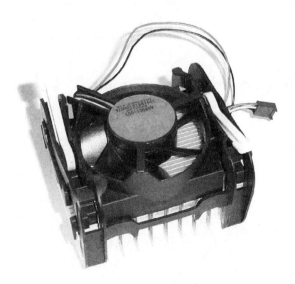

Figure 2-9
The mounting
bracket for the
Pentium 4 cooler

2. If the processor came with thermal tape, remove the backing. If not, spread a thin layer of thermal compound across the metal top of the processor.

3. Plug the fan's three-wire power lead into a nearby three-pin receptacle on the motherboard.

4. Place the heat sink over the processor into the motherboard bracket. Then, lower the fan bracket into place, snapping each corner down. Finally, set the two levers so that they lock into place with pressure on the CPU. It should look similar to Figure 2-10.

Installing an Athlon XP Cooler

Now let's focus on the Athlon cooler.

1. Check out the processor socket. Two sides of the socket will have protruding nodes, to which the heat sink's metal bracket will clip. Examine the bracket for the holes.

2. If the processor came with thermal tape, remove the backing. If not, drop a small amount of thermal paste onto the center of the processor.

Figure 2-10
A Pentium 4
cooler in place

3. Depending on the metal bracket, you may have to use your fingers (if it has a handle) or a screwdriver to fasten it down. See Figure 2-11.

4. Plug the fan's three-wire power lead into a nearby three-pin receptacle on the motherboard.

Figure 2-11
Connecting the
bracket of an Athlon
cooler to the socket

5. Set the cooler into place with the bracket lined up with the corresponding hooks on the socket. Lower the bare side of the bracket over the first hook. Then, press down the other side of the bracket with either a screwdriver (if there's a notch for it) or your fingers (if there's a small handle). You'll have to use firm, steady pressure. Carefully work the second bracket around the second hook on the socket. It should look like Figure 2-12.

The Memory

The system memory, or RAM (Random Access Memory), is where data is stored while the processor is working on it or after it has finished calculating. Memory performance is crucial to a speedy system. Slow memory can bottleneck the system and reduce the processor's effectiveness. Two types of memory are used in a system: *cache* and *main* memory.

Cache

The main memory isn't the only place from which the processor gets data. It also uses its own banks of storage, called *Level 1 (L1)* and *Level 2 (L2) cache*. Since the cache is right on the processor's die, the processor can access it faster than it can access the main memory.

Figure 2-12
An Athlon cooler mounted

Data is whisked from the main memory to the cache by the cache *controller*. The cache controller tries to predict what information the processor will ask for next. If the processor asks for that information, it's immediately available and the processor goes to work on it. This is called a *cache hit*. When the processor asks for information that's not loaded into cache, it's called a *cache miss*. Although RAM's getting faster, it still doesn't run nearly as fast as the processor. This is why cache hits are crucial to the speed of the system.

L2 cache differs from L1 cache in several ways. First, it's larger: current processors have 256K or 512K of L2 cache, and only 64K of L1 cache. Second, it takes a few nanoseconds longer to reach L2 cache. L2 cache is on the die with current processors, but it didn't used to be; in older PCs, it's on the motherboard, separate from main memory, and instead of running at the processor core speed like L1 and current L2 cache, it runs at the speed of the FSB.

Cache hits are vital to the speedy performance of a processor. It's always better to have the needed data right on the die than it is to have to fetch it across the FSB from main memory. No matter how fast the FSB or the memory of the computer, it can't beat the near instantaneous fulfillment of a cache hit.

What About Upgrading the Cache?

You can't upgrade your processor's cache, because the cache is an integral part of the chip itself. In earlier times, cache came in the form of socketed chips on the motherboard and could be added onto as needed. Cache has since been moved to the processor die.

Main Memory

Main memory is used for data storage. Programs drop data there that the processor needs to calculate, and the processor returns the results to memory for the program to use. In a nutshell, that's how the processor runs programs.

Memory comes in the form of modules called SIMMs, DIMMs, RIMMs, or something similar. The *IMM* portion stands for *Inline Memory Module*, and the three precursors are *Single*, *Double*, and *Rambus*, respectively. Memory is measured in megabytes or even gigabytes. Figure 2-13 shows a DDR memory module.

It's easy to get confused about what's in memory and what's in storage, the latter of which refers to hard disks, removable media, and optical drives. Memory and storage are different animals, however. Their characteristics are as follows:

Memory	Storage
Is *volatile*, meaning that it doesn't store data when powered down.	Is *nonvolatile*. It keeps data stored when powered down.

Memory	Storage
Comes in the form of chips on rectangular printed circuit boards.	Comes in the form of hard disk platters, floppy disks, CD-ROMs, DVD-ROMs, and other physical media.
Is used by the processor to run programs.	Is used to store data for the long term.
Is accessed much faster than storage.	Is accessed more slowly than memory.

As you can see, memory is quite different from storage. The hard drive is the primary storage device in a system. It contains metal platters, and data is written to it with a magnetic head.

System memory is also referred to as RAM. When you see the specifications of a computer, the list will include an amount of memory written as, say, "512MB RAM." Although many devices are randomly accessed, including most storage devices, the term *RAM* usually refers to system memory.

Types of Memory

Many types of memory have been used in computers throughout their development. Today, two types are common: high-speed, narrow bandwidth memory

Figure 2-13
A 184-pin DDR
memory module

manufactured by Rambus called RDRAM (Rambus Dynamic Random Access Memory), and high-bandwidth memory called DDR SDRAM (Double Data Rate Synchronous DRAM).

Rambus DRAM runs at higher frequencies than DDR memory. RDRAM is available at 800MHz, 1066MHz, and 1200MHz. Only certain Intel chipsets work with RDRAM, and it's more expensive than DDR memory. The various speeds are referred to as PC800, PC1066, and PC1200. Like DDR memory, RDRAM transfers data twice during each clock cycle.

DDR memory is available at effective speeds up to 400MHz, which is what you'll want to get. It's called both PC3200 and DDR400, depending on where you read it. 400MHz DDR memory actually runs at 200MHz, but it performs data transfers twice per clock cycle. DDR RAM is also available with effective frequencies of 266MHz (PC2100), 333MHz (PC2700), and at higher speeds than 400MHz, but current motherboards don't support anything higher than 400MHz.

Choosing Memory

For the sake of both cost effectiveness and performance, we recommend 400MHz DDR memory. All of the motherboards we recommend use DDR memory, so if you go with one of our recommendations you'll be prepared for high-speed, extremely efficient memory.

Memory comes on long, thin modules called DIMMs, or Dual Inline Memory Modules. You should buy one 512MB DIMM: motherboards come with a limited number of DIMM slots, so you can keep the extra slots free in case you wish to upgrade down the road. Windows XP and all current games run smoothly with 512MB of memory. With less, Windows tends to swap data to and from its paging file fairly often. More memory may never be used unless you use memory-intensive software such as video editors.

Be sure to use name-brand memory, such as that from Corsair, Mushkin, or Viking. Generic memory is often cheap and shoddy, and it won't allow you to run it as strenuously as name-brand memory. One of our favorite memory vendors, Crucial, isn't making 400MHz DDR at the time of this writing, though it might be available by the time you read this.

Another specification to look for is the *CAS (Column Access Strobe) latency*. The higher the latency, the longer memory takes to respond to data requests. Most DDR memory has a CAS latency time of 2.5 cycles. Simplified, this means that after the memory controller has tapped the memory for data from a certain address, it takes two and a half clock cycles for the memory to respond. The lower the CAS latency, the faster the memory.

Depending on your motherboard, you may be able to use the BIOS setup program to "force" the computer to run with a lower CAS latency time, but the PC might become unstable. See "BIOS Tweaking and Overclocking," later in the chapter.

Installing the Memory Modules

Handle the memory modules by the edges and be sure to be static-safe at all times. Memory chips are extremely sensitive to static discharge.

Watch the Contacts

Don't touch the metal contacts that connect one component to another, such as the contacts on a memory module on the side that slides into the motherboard slot. The oil on your fingers can impede good contact and cause all sorts of problems.

1. Memory modules have notches on the side with the metal pins that correspond to bumps in the memory sockets on a motherboard (see Figure 2-14). Look at your DIMM module. Then, locate the first socket (usually labeled DIMM1 or DIMM0) on the motherboard. Open the plastic clasps on either side of the socket.

2. Align the memory module with the notches on the DIMM facing the bumps in the bottom of the socket. Slide the DIMM straight down into the socket (see Figure 2-15).

Figure 2-14
Notice the notches on the memory module.

Figure 2-15
Seating a DIMM
module

3. Apply pressure evenly across the entire module until it snaps into
   place; the two plastic clasps should raise and close around the DIMM
   of their own accord. It's important to make sure the DIMM is firmly
   seated; if it's not, your computer won't boot up. A properly seated
   DIMM module is shown in Figure 2-16.

Figure 2-16
A DIMM module
properly seated

BIOS Tweaking and Overclocking

You can directly affect the performance of your PC, regardless of the specifications of the various parts, through *tweaking*, which is resetting values for the highest performance possible, and *overclocking*, which is forcing a processor or bus to run faster than its native clock frequency. A number of tweaks can be implemented in the computer's BIOS setup program. You'll need a video card before you can enter the BIOS setup program.

You invoke the BIOS setup program by powering up or restarting the computer, and during the POST screen (that's the screen with the white letters on a black background that counts up your memory and detects your IDE devices), pressing the appropriate key. Usually, it's DELETE, but some motherboards have you press F1, F2, or a combination of keys. Watch the POST screen for instructions to enter setup (Figure 2-17).

BIOS Tweaking

When you've invoked the setup program, you will be faced with either a menu of areas in which you can make changes or a page style display of various screens in which you can perform similar tweaks. Familiarize yourself with the locations of various settings by surfing around the BIOS setup program. The bottom of the

Figure 2-17
A post screen with instructions to enter the setup menu

screen usually contains instructions of how to navigate the setup program and how to alter values. Try out the following tweaks. Note that it's best to wait until your computer is completely built up so that after each tweak you can boot up the operating system and test your computer for stability.

Cutting Down on Startup Time

Find a value with a name like "Quick POST" or "Quick Power On Self Test." Enable it if it's not already enabled. This will cut down on the time that the POST screen is displayed before the BIOS starts the operating system. See Figure 2-18.

Then find the area with boot options. You can define the order in which devices are tapped by the BIOS when it looks for an operating system. The options might include the CD-ROM drive, a SCSI device, removable media such as a floppy drive, and various hard drives. Make the first hard drive, often referred to as something like "HDD 0," the first boot device. That'll cut down the amount of time the computer looks for your Windows installation.

Tweaking Memory Timings

Find an area of the BIOS that contains memory options such as CAS latency and DRAM command rate.

First, set CAS latency to 2 and load up the operating system. Run a benchmark or play a game to check the system's stability. If it runs okay without any

Figure 2-18
Enable the Quick
Power On Self Test

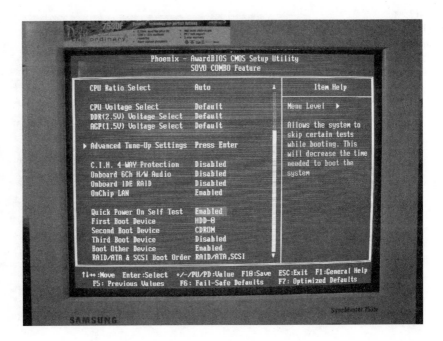

lockups or odd slowdowns, enter the BIOS setup again and change the DRAM command rate to 1 (Figure 2-19). Again, start up the operating system and test for stability.

If either setting causes a problem, reset it to its original value. These settings affect how memory is addressed and in changing them you're attempting to squeeze the utmost performance out of your system's memory.

Using Presets

Some BIOS setup utilities contain preset values for various speeds. Look for a setting labeled something like "System Performance" and check out its options. The options often include Normal, Failsafe, Fast, Fastest, and/or Turbo. Try setting the value at its fastest possible setting (Figure 2-20), and then enter the operating system to check for stability.

AGP Aperture Settings

The AGP aperture size specifies the amount of memory in which an AGP device can store graphics data. When the AGP controller queries an area in the AGP aperture range, data is transferred directly to the graphics device without bothering the processor. You'll want to set this to a minimum of 128MB (Figure 2-21). Few benchmarks show a difference between setting it there and at 256MB.

Figure 2-19
Set the DRAM command rate to 1 and test for stability.

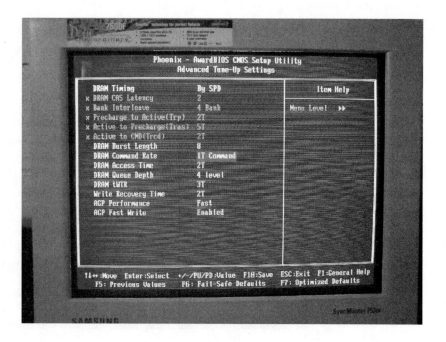

Figure 2-20
Try using high-speed
preset options.

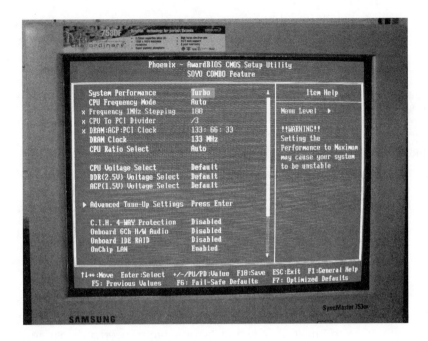

Overclocking

Imagine you're driving around in a car. As you cruise the highways, there's
nothing stopping you from blowing past the speed limit and driving 80 or 90

Figure 2-21
Set the AGP aperture
size to 128MB or
256MB.

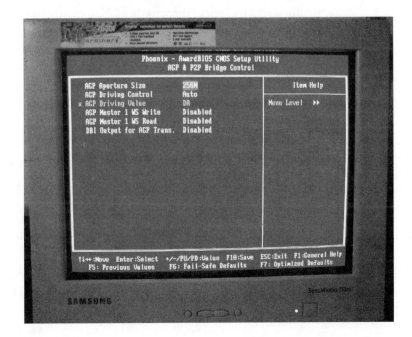

miles per hour. Sure, there's the threat that you'll get pulled over and lose your license, and your car's engine is only powerful enough to reach a certain speed. Plus, pushing your vehicle to perform faster than its makers had in mind will increase the wear and tear it suffers.

What Can Happen with Overclocking?

Overclocking your processor can void warranties and prematurely age, or even damage, your equipment. Overclocking pushes your equipment past its specified operating parameters. It increases the amount of heat your components generate and can lead your gear toward an early death.

In a similar vein, you can push your processor to perform past its specification. Through the popular action known as *overclocking*, you can push your machine to find its true limits, though not without some risk to your components. Some folks see overclocking as a free upgrade: getting a 1.5GHz processor to run at 1.7GHz boosts the system speed, not to mention the overclocker's ego.

Indeed, overclocking is such a popular pastime for do-it-yourselfers that it's cultured a massive community on the Internet, with dozens of web sites dedicated to the practice. They're stocked with how-to guides, features discussing new and current processor technology, day-to-day industry news, and burgeoning message boards full of mostly friendly users who swap anecdotes, victories, warnings, and technical information. You can even find books on overclocking.

The ability to overclock processors is strongly dependant on the system's motherboard. Some motherboards offer little or no control over bus or multiplier settings, while others give you full control over those and even voltage settings. Note that Intel and AMD lock the multiplier settings within their chips, but AMD processors can be unlocked (see Figure 2-22).

Overclocking Intel Processors

You will need a motherboard that allows you to change the bus settings in small increments.

On current systems, the bus's native frequency will be 100MHz for a 400MHz FSB and 133MHz for a 533MHz FSB. (During normal operation, the bus is "quad pumped" to reach the higher frequencies.) Some motherboards let you increase the bus speed, which forces the processor to work at a higher frequency.

If you have an overclocking-friendly motherboard, you do the dirty work in the BIOS setup. Some manufacturers, like SOYO, ABIT, and ASUS, have a special

Figure 2-22
Many BIOS setup
programs let you bus
overclock the system.

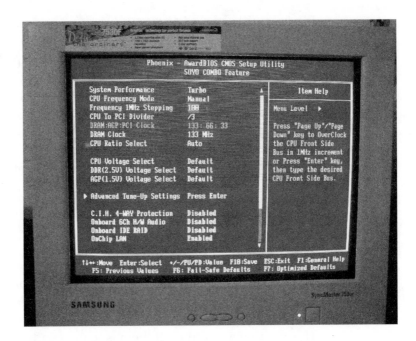

page in the BIOS setup menu just for overclocking and performance tweaking your system.

To give you an example of bus overclocking, a Pentium 4 2.4GHz machine runs on a 133MHz bus with a 533MHz FSB. To get to 2.4GHz, the 133MHz is set with a multiplier of 18x. The multiplier is locked. Raising the bus speed, while keeping the multiplier the same, forces the CPU to work faster.

Bus Speed, MHz	Multiplier	CPU Speed, MHz
133	18	2400
134	18	2412
135	18	2430
136	18	2448
137	18	2466
138	18	2484
139	18	2502
140	18	2520

When you overclock the FSB, you have to watch that you're not pushing the PCI bus or the AGP bus too hard. Whether you can overclock the FSB separately from those other buses depends upon the capabilities of the motherboard.

It's helpful to use a benchmarking program, such as Bapco's *SYSmark* or FutureMark.com's *PCMark*, to see the results of your work. Be sure to run the benchmark before you begin your overclocking experiment to get a baseline, and then benchmark each increment you overclock.

It's also helpful to run a utility that monitors the heat of your processor. Intel provides one for free. It's vitally important to understand that, by overclocking, you increase the heat that your processor generates and you can easily age or damage the processor if you push it too hard.

If your computer hangs, reboots spontaneously, or if you start getting jillions of errors while running Windows and applications, back down the bus speed until the system is stable.

Overclocking AMD Processors

Athlon processors can be bus overclocked just like Pentiums. However, it's possible to unlock the multiplier on some AMD processors. This involves bridging a set of four tiny contacts. They're called the L1 bridges, and they can be found on the top of the processor.

The easiest way to connect them is to use conductive paint, and draw a line from each contact to its opposite mate. It's very important that you connect only the opposite pins to each other, and avoid connecting adjacent pins to each other. If you connect adjacent pins, you could short out part of the processor.

More recent Athlons have made it much more difficult to connect the L1 bridges. Using a laser beam, they've cut a divot in the motherboard between the contacts, and it can't be bridged with conductive ink or paint. Various overclocking web sites suggest various ways to work around this, such as filling in the divots with a nonconductive heat sink compound and then bridging the gaps.

Is it worth the trouble when you can perform bus overclocking without worrying about the L1 bridges? Yes and no: While there's the danger of shorting out your processor if you screw up and connect adjacent bridges, multiplier overclocking is gentler to the overall system as overclocks affect only the CPU, and not any related buses. However, you can bus overclock without fear of damaging your processor by shorting out the L1 bridges.

Typically, the most successful overclocking sees a maximum of only a 10 percent performance increase. You can also overclock your video card to increase 3-D gaming performance (see Chapter 4). Whether you overclock is up to you. There's a lot of good information on the web at sites like *www.hardocp.com*, *extremeoverclocking.com*, *www.tweaktown.com*, and many more. Most of these sites offer forums where you can communicate with the overclockers' community at large, which is full of friendly and mostly knowledgeable people whose need for speed is palpable.

Multiprocessing

It's possible to build a system with more than one processor. *SMP* (*Symmetrical Multiprocessing*) systems are usually used as servers and as high-performance workstations for CAD (Computer Aided Design), 3-D rendering, PhotoShop editing, and other severely processor-dependent tasks.

However, if your pocketbook is wide and you want the ultimate in workstation performance, an SMP system may be right for you. In an SMP system, multithreaded applications get a boost as processes are sent to each processor, so the two CPUs work in unison to run programs.

XP and SMP

Windows XP Home doesn't support SMP. If you wish to use SMP with Windows XP, you'll need Windows XP Professional. However, some games don't run on XP Professional.

To implement an SMP system similar to the way we've set up a single-processor PC thus far, you'll need a special motherboard with two CPU sockets, a compatible version of Windows such as Windows 2000 or Windows XP Professional, two processors, and memory.

Intel and AMD both make special processors dedicated to SMP processing. Intel manufactures the Xeon DP (for dual-processor systems), currently topping out at 2.8GHz, and the Xeon MP (for multiprocessor systems) at speeds up to 2GHz. AMD creates the Athlon MP, currently available as fast as the 2600+.

The ideal chipset for an Intel solution is the i7505 chipset, created by Intel. It uses a memory technology called *dual channel DDR,* which effectively doubles the bandwidth compared to traditional DDR. This new technology is just emerging as this book is being written.

Note that doubling the number of processors doesn't equate to doubling the performance of a comparable single-processor system. Dual processors share the same memory and FSB. There's a significant performance increase, especially if you run processor-intensive applications such as movie encoders, 3-D rendering applications, CAD, and so on.

You get the best results from SMP-aware applications, but any multithreaded game or application can benefit from an SMP setup.

The Hardware

For an Intel solution, the Iwill DPL533 motherboard supports dual Xeon DP processors. Based on the Intel E7505 chipset, it offers a wide range of features, including a 533MHz FSB and 8X AGP.

More cost effective is an AMD solution. A motherboard like Tyan's Thunder K7X Pro (S2469), based on AMD's 760 MPX chipset, is a perfect platform for dual Athlon MP 2600+ processors.

In each case, you'll need 512MB of DDR266 memory.

Install the motherboard, the processors, and the memory in the same manner discussed earlier in the chapter with single-processor systems. The only difference you'll face is that you have to install a pair of processors and heat sinks.

Whether you're using a single or dual processor system, you're now ready for the next step. Chapter 3 discusses the visual part of your gaming experience: the graphics card.

Chapter 3
The Graphics Card

Tools of the Trade

A medium Philips head screwdriver

You've got the core of your system built; now it's time to give it a soul. The graphics card is the pivotal part that differentiates a high-end gaming system from a listless wanna-be. Current 3-D games need not only powerful CPUs, efficient motherboards, and lightning-fast memory, but they also require a kick-ass 3-D processor that crunches the polygons and textures that paint the game world.

The market for graphics cards, also called video cards, is complex and confusing. You must choose from a wide array of cards based on a number of current- and last-generation chipsets. Most chipset families complicate the matter further by offering cutting-edge, mid-range and budget parts aimed at different market segments. Of course, you'll want to focus on the highest performance products available, as they're aimed squarely at performance-hungry gamers.

Currently, 3-D graphics are ahead of the technology curve. Late-generation products support features that have yet to appear in actual games—and probably won't appear until late 2003 or early 2004. In addition to feature sets, various graphics cards offer different levels of pure polygon-pumping muscle that directly affects the performance of current 3-D titles.

APIs, Chipsets, and Cards

In choosing a graphics card, you'll be faced with a dictionary's worth of mumbo jumbo that we'll help you understand. Based on the e-mail that this author receives, the most confusing aspects of the decision process is figuring out the difference between 3-D APIs, 3-D chipsets, and graphics cards themselves.

3-D APIs

API stands for *application programming interface*. At its most basic, it's a software layer that makes hardware, software, and the operating system compatible with one another. An API provides programmers with a set of common, compatible instructions so that they don't have to bother with programming to specific cards and chipsets; as long as they program to an API, they theoretically don't have to deal with the rigors of making their software compatible with all the hardware that's available, or with the operating system itself.

For example, if a programmer writes to a 3-D hardware API such as Microsoft's Direct3D, he shouldn't have to worry about his program's compatibility with all of the different Direct3D-compliant graphics cards that are available. Similarly, if a graphics card manufacturer builds its hardware with Direct3D-compatible parts and drivers, it shouldn't have to worry about compatibility with Direct3D-compliant programs. An API smoothes the way for both sides.

It would be terrific if that theory held up in practice, but incompatibilities creep up in even the best laid programs. Good game companies put their wares through countless hours of compatibility testing on the vast majority of computer hardware in circulation. Even so, games are often released with incompatibilities that the programmers didn't know about when the game shipped. These are usually addressed in *patches*, which are downloadable updates to their products.

Two major 3-D APIs are in use today: OpenGL and Direct3D.

OpenGL

Developed by Silicon Graphics, Inc., OpenGL is widely used by 3-D modelers for high-end business applications. When John Carmac optioned to use OpenGL for the first 3-D accelerated version of *Quake* (commonly called *GLQuake*), OpenGL was embraced by the gaming community and is used by many game developers today. The current version of OpenGL is version 1.3.

Direct3D/DirectX

Part of Microsoft's DirectX library of APIs, Direct3D is more popular among game developers for 3-D programming—but getting there took a while. Early versions of DirectX were widely considered incomplete and difficult to program to. By the time DirectX 5 came out, Direct3D had evolved into a feature-rich, programmer-friendly API, and with each incarnation of DirectX it's gotten better.

Both OpenGL 1.3 and DirectX 8.1 are supported by virtually every graphics card available on the market today, so you don't have to worry about checking for compatibility before you purchase a card. The latest version of Direct3D, part of DirectX 9's library, is supported by only the very latest graphics hardware.

Chipsets

Like motherboards, all graphics cards are based on one or another *chipset*. The chipset incorporates the logic on the graphics card, including the *graphics processing unit (GPU)*, which does the grunt work of creating 3-D graphics. The chipset determines such factors as the APIs with which the card is compatible, how much video memory it supports, its Accelerated Graphics Port (AGP) support, and the clock frequencies of the core logic and the memory.

Companies such as ATI, Nvidia, and SiS create graphics chipsets and license them to final market card manufacturers. Nvidia and SiS don't market cards to the public; they only create chipsets. Another manufacturer, Matrox, makes its own chipsets and cards. ATI makes chipsets and cards, and it also licenses its chipsets to other manufacturers to make cards. It's a bit confusing; Table 3-1 should help.

Manufacturer	Makes Chipsets	Makes Cards Based on Its Chipsets	Licenses Its Chipsets
ATI	Yes	Yes	Yes
Matrox	Yes	Yes	No
Nvidia	Yes	No	Yes
SiS	Yes	No	Yes

Table 3-1
Chipsets Makers' Roles in the Graphics Card Industry

Cards

Graphics cards themselves are made by a huge variety of manufacturers. The players include ATI, Matrox, ASUS, Crucial, Gigabyte, MSI, Leadtek, PNY, and ABIT.

Card manufacturers license chipsets from chipset manufacturers (except in the case of ATI and Matrox, who make their own chipsets). Cards are produced based on a particular chipset. Some card manufacturers stick very close to the *reference design*, or the sample cards created by the chipset manufacturers, while others take liberties with their drivers' capabilities or the configurations of their cards. For the most part, though, the chipset determines the speed and feature set of the card. For instance, a PNY card based on the Nvidia GeForce4 Ti 4600 chipset performs almost identically to an ABIT card based on the same chipset.

The major differences between cards based on the same chipset isn't performance—it's the price, availability, and warranty offered by the card manufacturer. The price range is determined by a chipset (for instance, the GeForce Ti 4600 is available on cards ranging from $200 to $300), but the card manufacturer determines any variance within that range. Usually, you'll want to decide on a chipset first, and then you can check to see what card manufacturers have to offer with your chosen chipset.

The Players

It's the chipset that makes a graphics card what it is, and it's the chipset manufacturers that makes PC enthusiasts excited when a new product is announced or released. Graphics chipset makers are almost always ahead of the technology curve, offering exciting new features sometimes months before games start to incorporate them. Even so, newer chipsets also offer raw oomph, pushing current and older games to higher *frame rates*.

Frame rate is king. The frame rate is the number of still screens that the graphics card displays on the monitor per second, creating the illusion of animation. This rate determines how smooth a game looks while you're playing it. The threshold of playability is about 25 frames per second (fps). A rate of 30fps is good, and 60fps is ideal. Though it's nice to have an even higher frame rate, your brain can't tell the difference once the frame rate rises above 60fps.

So why should you want a graphics card with a chipset that runs games at 100fps? The answer lies in features: if the card is that powerful, you can turn on such features as anti-aliasing (discussed in its own section a little later in this chapter) and *anisotropic filtering* (a graphics technique that keeps textures crisp on objects that trail off in the distance from the point of view), and you can increase the game's resolution while still maintaining a frame rate at, or above, 60fps.

Four major players currently compete in the graphics chipset market: ATI, Nvidia, Matrox, and SiS. They are discussed here, along with 3dfx graphics chipsets, which, while no longer available, were important players at one time. We don't include information about chipsets that come with motherboards, because they usually offer lackluster graphics acceleration. Onboard graphics adapters are good for servers and business workstations, but as a proud gamer you'll want the cutting edge in performance.

ATI

ATI has been in the graphics business for years. In terms of 3-D performance, it often played second fiddle to Nvidia, which has usually had better, faster, and newer graphics hardware available. That was true even up to ATI's last generation of products, the Radeon 8000 family. The 8500 was a great card, but it spent a very short time at the top of the graphics chipset heap before Nvidia shut it out.

That all changed with the ATI Radeon 9700 Pro (shown in Figure 3-1). Released in mid-2002, it's held the crown of the graphics industry into 2003. It's got everything a gamer needs: fierce power, plenty of features, and competitive pricing. A DirectX 9–compliant part even before DirectX 9 was released, it's well ahead of current gaming technology, and ready for next generation titles that won't be available for a long time.

Figure 3-1
ATI's Radeon 9700 Pro

ATI only recently started licensing its chipsets to other graphics card makers. Until that time, its own cards were the only platforms for its chipsets. By selling its chipsets to other companies, ATI has done something wonderful for gamers: it has created competition between card manufacturers and driven down the price of its products. The Radeon 9700 Pro came out with a price tag of about $400; at the time of this writing, *www.Pricewatch.com* lists the cards for as little as $230.

The Radeon 9000 family also includes mainstream chipsets, the Radeon 9500 Pro and the Radeon 9500, which are available with a street price of around $175 and $120, respectively. Its current budget chipsets, the Radeon 9000 Pro and Radeon 9000, are featured on cards available for less than $100.

Nvidia

This long-standing king of the graphics industry was usurped by ATI in 2002. Its GeForce4 Ti series, with its high-end Ti 4600, is still an excellent range of graphical chipsets, but Nvidia can no longer claim that it offers the fastest solution on the block.

That could change, though. The GeForce FX, the latest offering from Nvidia, was poised to roll out in early 2003. Its release probably took place between the time that this was written and the time this book hit the store shelves. History has shown that Nvidia's offerings are fast, stable, and ready for the latest in gaming technology.

Nvidia came into its own in the late 1990s,, when it pulled the rug of the graphics acceleration business out from under 3dfx's feet. Nvidia's TNT series had the audacity to match 3dfx's performance, and the early GeForce-based cards actually outpaced the best that 3dfx had to offer. Until ATI stole the crown, Nvidia was on top. Figure 3-2 shows an Nvidia-based graphics card.

Figure 3-2
An ASUS graphics card based on the GeForce4 4600

One of Nvidia's strengths is its driver support. A dedicated software team churns out new device drivers for the Nvidia chipsets on a regular basis, and each driver release usually ekes out even more performance from the chipset. ATI has, until recently, been lacking in that area.

Matrox

Once a major player in the 3-D graphics industry, Matrox has taken a backseat to Nvidia and ATI. Its Mystique and M3D cards were gems in the mid-to-late 1990s, but with its shift to its Millennium line it gradually faded into the background. Today, Matrox cards are better suited for workstations than for gaming.

Matrox tried to make a comeback with its Parhelia graphics card in mid-2002. Although its specs looked promising, the card's performance proved to be lackluster compared to parts based on late-model ATI and Nvidia chipsets. Its major claim to fame is "surround gaming," enabled by its unique support for three displays. However, only a handful of games supports surround gaming, and the technology has failed to make waves in the gaming market.

SiS

A fairly recent combatant in the 3-D acceleration arena, SiS's latest chipsets travel under the moniker Xabre. The latest Xabre is the Xabre 600, a follow up to the Xabre 400 (shown in Figure 3-3).

Figure 3-3
A SiS Xabre 400
reference card

The Xabre family attempts to be a full-featured, AGP 8X, DirectX 9 group of chipsets available at a budget price. Unfortunately, Xabre chipsets perform like budget parts, so they're unable to compete with current-generation solutions from Nvidia and ATI. As such, SiS's graphics chipsets have made little headway in capturing the market from the two major powerhouses.

Due to their lackluster performance, we don't recommend cards based on Xabre chipsets.

Gone but Not Forgotten: 3dfx

3dfx is out of business. Why do we include it here? Because it paved the way for 3-D gaming as it stands today.

3dfx's Voodoo Graphics chipset, released in 1997 and available at the time on a huge variety of cards, was the first truly powerful 3-D accelerator. Before Voodoo Graphics, 3-D acceleration was mired in proprietary APIs, 3-D games were generally released with software-based 3-D engines, and special hardware accelerated versions of the games were bundled with 3-D cards. It was difficult to find an off-the-shelf game that featured a hardware assisted 3-D engine. All too often, 3-D games actually ran more slowly on 3-D hardware than they did in software.

The Voodoo Graphics chipset, with its own OpenGL-derived API, Glide, brought raw power to the mix. Embraced by Id Software for *GLQuake*, the Voodoo Graphics chipset was widely accepted by gamers and managed to secure a respectable install base, big enough for Glide to take off as the most supported 3-D API of its time.

Both the Voodoo Graphics chipset and its follow-up, the Voodoo2, were designed for graphics add-on cards. They worked in conjunction with a 2-D/3-D card and were unable to dish out 2-D graphics, such as a Windows desktop, on their own. Subsequent chipsets, the Voodoo3 and Voodoo4/5, were full-featured AGP solutions that didn't need another graphics card in the system.

3dfx continued to produce cutting-edge graphics technology until it sold out to Nvidia and went out of business in late 2000. 3dfx may not be around anymore, but it's undeniable that it paved the way for 3-D gaming as we enjoy it today.

Features

When you encounter a graphics card, be it on the web or in a store, you're faced with a barrage of 3-D terminology and glossy marketing monikers describing the card's features. Unfortunately, few definitions are given, so to many confused gamers it comes off as a lot of mystical mumbo jumbo.

AGP Modes

Speedy AGP is important. It allows for a direct pipeline between the graphics card and the computer's main memory. AGP lets video data that won't fit into a graphics card's local memory be stored into the aperture space in the system's own bank of memory.

ATI's Radeon 9700 and 9500 series, Nvidia's NV18-based GeForce4 MX440, its NV28-based GeForce4 Ti 4200, and its GeForce FX series all support AGP 8X. AGP 8X, also known as AGP 3.0, is the fastest current AGP speed available. For it to function, both a compliant graphics card and motherboard are required.

Other graphics equipment, such as ATI Radeon 9000 chipsets and those based on the Nvidia GeForce4 Ti 4600, are AGP 4X compliant. That does not mean they're half as fast overall as their AGP 8X counterparts; it means that video data has half the bus bandwidth to swap data from system memory.

Dual-Display Support

Both ATI and Nvidia cards offer support for a pair of displays. Nvidia calls its dual-display support Nview, while ATI refers to the same concept as HydraVision. Dual displays allow you, for example, to display one application on one monitor and the other on a second display, to watch a DVD on a TV while crunching a spreadsheet on a monitor, or to stretch the Windows desktop across two displays.

Anti-Aliasing

Anti-aliasing, also called full-scene anti-aliasing (FSAA), is a method of blending the colors at the edges of textures or polygons to eliminate jagged diagonal lines and artifacts that they cause, like shimmering distance textures. Early forms of anti-aliasing carried a high performance overhead, greatly reducing games' frame rates. They also notoriously blurred the edges of textures and polygons, reducing the sharpness of the game scene.

Current cards have the muscle to allow gamers to turn on anti-aliasing while keeping the frame rates playable. They also provide sharper, more accurate scenes than early anti-aliasing techniques could provide. Nvidia calls its latest anti-aliasing technology Intellisample Technology. ATI calls its current anti-aliasing technique SmoothVision 2.0.

Filtering

Similar to anti-aliasing, *filtering* is used to blend textures to reduce blockiness and pixilation and to smooth transitions between textures as they move nearer to, or farther from, the point of view (MIP mapping).

Three types of filtering can be used: bilinear, trilinear, and anisotropic. Bilinear filtering blends flat textures from a two-dimensional point of view. Trilinear filtering adds a z value, which helps smooth the transition between *MIP maps*. MIP mapping involves using less-detailed textures as an object gets farther from the viewpoint, similar to what the human eye does when viewing distances. Anisotropic filtering can be used with bilinear or trilinear filtering, and it increases the filtering precision by using a wider range of *texels* (textured pixels).

Both ATI and Nvidia allow you to force anisotropic filtering through their driver interfaces. ATI's driver interface allows you to set the level of anisotropic filtering from 2X to 16X, while Nvidia's GeForce 4 and earlier chipset's drivers allow you to force anisotropic filtering only from 2X to 8X. We have yet to see the GeForce FX or its driver interface.

Programmable Shaders

A relatively recent feature in 3-D graphics chipsets, programmable pixel and vertex shaders allow programmers to create blazingly realistic lighting effects of their own design. Programmers are no longer limited to the lighting effects included with Direct3D, as they can create their own routines in assembly language to achieve any effect they desire. ATI calls its programmable shaders SmartShaders, and they're currently in their second incarnation (SmartShader 2.0). Nvidia calls its shaders the infinite FX II Engine for its GeForce4 Ti parts, and CineFX for the GeForce FX.

Choosing a Graphics Card

Graphics technology is still evolving at a ridiculously fast pace. Nvidia has made a habit of releasing new products or refreshes of current products every six months. ATI unleashes a new architecture about once per year, and it trickles out twists on that architecture for several months after.

The graphics card affects your gaming experience more noticeably than the system's processor. You'd notice a bigger difference in frame rates between a current generation and a last generation video card than you would between two processors within a few hundred clock frequencies of each other.

The ATI Radeon 9700 Pro is a work of art. Fitted with 128MB of Double Data Rate (DDR) memory, it blasts through pixels and polygons at stunning speeds and runs every current game with high visual quality settings at excellent frame rates. ATI's driver support has gone from lackluster to exemplary in the past couple of years. Prepare to pay $250 to $300 for a card based on this chipset.

If that's not in your price range, the Radeon 9500 Pro is a mid-priced card with largely the same feature set as the 9700 Pro. The biggest difference between the two is horsepower: the 9500 Pro benchmarks slower than its big brother.

Both cards are DirectX 9 parts, fully compliant with the latest version of Microsoft's multimedia driver library. That means that with one or the other, you'll be ready for DirectX 9 games when they start trickling to market—which, as of this writing, is probably late 2003.

Having yet to test Nvidia's GeForce FX line, we can't recommend it. However, Nvidia's track record is remarkable. Each new architecture it's released has always been well ahead of the last. Furthermore, like the Radeon 9700 Pro and 9500 Pro, the GeForce FX is slated to be a DirectX 9–compliant part. Nvidia's driver support has always been stellar. Watch sites like *www.extremetech.com* and *www.gamersdepot.com* for reviews of GeForce FX products when they come out, and adjust your selection accordingly.

As for cards themselves, it's often hard to distinguish one card from the next, provided they're based on the same chipset. A few manufacturers add more powerful cooling solutions, making overclocking easier. ASUS, which makes Nvidia-based graphics cards, is known for this. Crucial, which makes a Radeon 9700 Pro–based card, offers a lifetime warranty with its products (Figure 3-4).

Figure 3-4
Crucial's Radeon 9700 Pro is all but identical to ATI's own card based on its flagship chipset.

Choose your chipset first. Then shop around for the secondary features you prefer and the price you're willing to pay. The web site *www.pricewatch.com* is an excellent and popular resource for finding the best deal on a given chipset.

Installing a Graphics Card

Installing a graphics card is a simple affair. If you've installed a PCI card or even an ancient ISA card, it will be old hat. Don't forget to be static-safe! See Chapter 2 to learn how to handle sensitive equipment, such as a graphics card, safely.

1. Open up your system. Locate the AGP slot (Figure 3-5); it's usually a brown slot between the row of white PCI slots and the processor.

Figure 3-5
An AGP slot

2. Locate the contacts on the graphics card (Figure 3-6). The contacts will slide neatly down into the slot.

Figure 3-6
The contacts of an AGP card

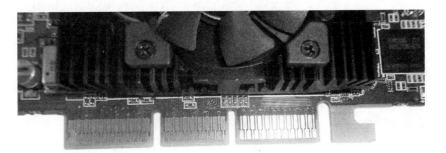

3. Remove the metal cover that corresponds with the AGP slot from the back of the PC by removing its screw and popping it out. Slide the graphics card carefully into place, with the metal gate taking the place of the cover you removed. Apply firm pressure evenly across the card until it's completely seated, as seen in Figure 3-7. Then, replace the screw to secure the AGP card in place.

Figure 3-7
Installing
an AGP card

Updating the Drivers

Just as it's important to keep your motherboard drivers up-to-date, it's vital that you keep your video card drivers up-to-date. You can use the drivers provided by your card manufacturer, but sometimes they lag behind updates that ship directly from chipset makers. Drivers from chipset makers are called *reference drivers*, and it's best to use them when they're ahead of the drivers offered by the card manufacturer.

You can acquire reference drivers by heading directly to the chipset makers' web sites, such as *www.nvidia.com* and *www.ati.com*, depending on the chipset of your graphics card. Head to the tech support or driver download link on the main page and follow the instructions to download the proper driver for your operating system. Your download will come in the form of an executable file. Driver installations are automatic: just run the executable that you download and the installation program will take care of the rest.

ATI Driver Controls

ATI throws in a curve by packaging the driver control program separately from the drivers themselves. Without the driver control program, you can't adjust things like anti-aliasing and anisotropic filtering. The driver control program is usually packaged with driver updates, but ATI recently began packaging it separately. Watch the ATI web site for updates of both drivers and the driver control interface.

Follow news sites like *www.bluesnews.com* or make regular visits to your chipset manufacturer's web site to keep your drivers current. New drivers often squeeze more performance out of your graphics hardware. They also contain bug fixes, compatibility updates, and other important bits of code.

Some sites, like *www.3dchipset.com*, offer graphics device drivers that are still in beta form. Use them with caution, because beta drivers usually haven't been tested with a wide variety of applications. If you use beta drivers, you may see performance gains or losses compared to the current final reference drivers. You may also experience incompatibilities in the form of graphical glitches, crashing games, system hangs, or spontaneous reboots. You can always install final drivers over beta drivers to restore stability.

Gauging Your Performance: Benchmarking Your Graphics Card

While it's nice to play games that run smoothly at high frame rates, it's somehow nicer to put a number on your gaming machine's prowess. That's what benchmarks are for. Benchmarking a graphics card with various settings enabled gives you an idea of how well your card can run games with the conditions you set for the benchmark. Want to see how big of a performance hit that 4X anti-aliasing causes? Benchmark it. Wondering how well your rig does at lofty resolutions like 1600×1200? Benchmark it.

Two types of benchmarks are used:

❑ **Synthetic benchmarks**   Run theoretical simulations through the system and spit out arbitrary numbers or scores

❑ **Real-world benchmarks**   Actual games that include a routine in which you can run a segment of a game (a demo) to get a score in frames per second

Benchmarking Guidelines

When you benchmark your graphics card, you should follow a few simple guidelines to ensure that you get accurate, repeatable results. Controlled testing conditions will give you the best and most useful benchmarks.

❑ Don't run any programs in the background. Shut down any application that's open before you run a test.

❑ Reboot in between benchmarks, and don't run anything you don't have to after you reboot and before you run the benchmark.

❑ For each set of testing conditions, run each benchmark three to five times and average the results.

❑ Don't make any changes to other aspects of the system between benchmarks.

❑ To compare one piece of hardware to another (for instance, to compare two graphics cards), run them on the same system with the same parameters, changing nothing except the hardware you're comparing.

Here's an example: Let's say you're comparing the performance of your graphics card before and after you update its drivers. First, you'd run several benchmarks with the old drivers. Then, *without changing anything else, including the resolution, anti-aliasing settings, other display settings, any other drivers, and so on,* run another set of benchmarks with the new graphics card drivers. If you change anything but the graphics card drivers, the comparison between the two driver revisions won't be accurate.

Try benchmarking at different resolutions and with different features enabled to get a feel for how well your system runs games under different conditions. You should see decent scores with the details turned up.

Graphics Benchmark Programs

The industry-standard benchmark is called 3DMark2001 SE. However, it's a synthetic benchmark using theoretical game environments, so it's not often used exclusively. Instead, it's used with a number of real games that contain frame counters, which are employed to process prerecorded demos and measure how fast your computer is able to display them. Some games, such as Novalogic's *Comanche 4* and Epic's *Unreal Tournament 2003*, contain easy-to-run benchmarks, while others require you to input various commands manually to run their benchmarks.

3DMark2001 SE

This synthetic benchmark is widely used in graphics and system hardware reviews across the industry. A free version is available for download at *www.futuremark.com*. It contains a number of tests that use both gamelike environments and purely synthetic throughput and video processing tests to spit out a final, total score, and individual test results.

The easiest way to use 3DMark is simply to start the program and click the Benchmark button. It'll run its suite of benchmarks at a resolution of 1024×768 at 32-bit color. If you wish to change anything, such as enabling anti-aliasing, you can click a Change button.

Comanche 4

This Direct3D-accelerated game features a free benchmark that you can download from *www.novalogic.com*. A helicopter simulator (or *sim* for short), the game pushes large numbers of polygons and textures through the pipe while using pixel shaders for shading and lighting duties.

It's very easy to use (Figure 3-8). Simply navigate through the Start menu to the Novalogic folder, and click the *Comanche 4* Demo Benchmark Test. Select a resolution, a color depth, and any other options you desire. You should elect to disable vsync so that the benchmark score isn't limited to your monitor's refresh rate.

Using Vsync

When you're not benchmarking, if the frame rate of a game is higher than a monitor's vertical refresh rate, graphical irregularities will appear on the screen. Use the vsync option in your card's driver Setup menu to synchronize the game's frame rate and the monitor's vertical refresh rate.

Figure 3-8
Comanche 4 is a DirectX 8.1 game with beautiful lighting effects.

Unreal Tournament 2003

Another game with an easily accessible benchmark, *Unreal Tournament 2003* (Figure 3-9) is a relatively recent game that features a late generation 3-D engine that strains any system. The benchmark runs two modes, flyby and botmatch, each of which stresses the system with scads of polygons, textures, and special effects.

To run the *UT 2003* benchmark, navigate to the game's *SYSTEM* directory and find the file called *benchmark.exe*. Choose your resolution and let the system do the rest. When the benchmark is complete, it returns a score for both its flyby and its botmatch modes.

Figure 3-9
Unreal Tournament 2003 features a sexy engine that strains any system.

Serious Sam: The Second Encounter

Croteam's frenetic sequel to the *Doom*-style sensation features a beast of a game engine and cutting-edge graphics (see Figure 3-10). Here's how to run a benchmark:

1. Navigate through the Options menu to Video Options, and adjust the graphical settings as you wish. You'll find more graphics settings, such as bilinear/trilinear filtering settings, in the Advanced Options menu.

2. Then pull down the console by pressing the apostrophe (`) key. Type **/dem_bProfile=1** and press ENTER. Press the apostrophe key (`) again to close the console.

3. Finally, open the Demos menu. Select the Cooperative demo for the best taste of what your graphics card can do.

4. When the demo finishes running, pull down the console to find the average fps score.

Figure 3-10
Serious Sam:
The Second Encounter
uses OpenGL to
accelerate it's
visceral world.

Jedi Knight II: Jedi Outcast

This popular *Star Wars* game is based on the OpenGL-accelerated *Quake 3 Arena* engine. It represents a sweeping update of the engine, offering new effects, more detailed models, and other new twists (see Figure 3-11).

1. Run the multiplayer executable. Before you run the benchmark, make a stop in the System menu and set up the graphical options to suit your needs. You need to jump through a few flaming hoops to run the benchmark.

2. Pull down the console by holding SHIFT and pressing the apostrophe (`). Type **devmap ffa_bespin** and then press ENTER. A multiplayer map will load.

3. Pull down the console again, if necessary, and enter **timedemo 1** and then **disconnect**. The map will close.

4. Finally, enter **demo jk2ffa** in the console and the demo will run. When it's over, pull down the console and press the PAGE UP key to scroll upward until you see a score in fps.

Figure 3-11
Jedi Knight II: Jedi Outcast is based on the Quake 3 Arena engine.

Tweaking Features

Most graphics cards give you control over their feature sets so you can adjust them for a nice mix of visual quality and high-frame-rate playability. Furthermore, games themselves usually offer various display modes to help you further tailor your experience in specific titles.

Change the graphics card settings by right-clicking an empty portion of the Windows desktop. Click Properties in the pop-up menu to open the Display Properties window shown in Figure 3-13. Select the Settings tab, and then click the Advanced button.

Figure 3-12
Display Properties
window

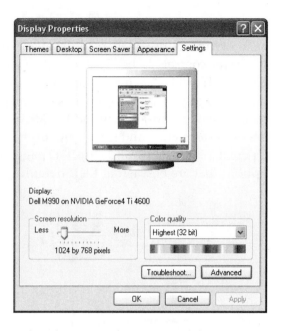

With an ATI-based Radeon 9500/9700, some of the tabs in the next dialog will
look like those shown in Figure 3-13. You can adjust settings for OpenGL and
Direct3D accelerated games separately. Adjustable settings include anti-aliasing
(2X to 6X), anisotropic filtering (2X to 16X), texture detail levels and MIP mapping levels (both carry a range, balancing performance and quality), and vsync
(off or on).

Figure 3-13
ATI's OpenGL
Properties sheet;
the Direct3D sheet
is nearly identical.

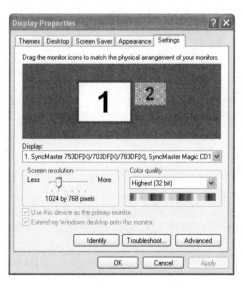

Nvidia's interface used to resemble ATI's, but recently Nvidia revamped it, as shown in Figure 3-14. We didn't have a GeForce FX to play with, but we expect its driver controls to be similar to the GeForce4 family's. When you click the GeForce Ti 4x00 tab, a menu pops out of the side. It includes a performance and quality page, which lets you tweak overall performance (application preference to aggressive), anti-aliasing (off to 4XS, a special Direct3D-only mode that balances performance and visual quality), and anisotropic filtering (off to 8X). OpenGL (Figure 3-15) and Direct3D pages let you tweak vsync and a few other options that are best left at their default settings.

Figure 3-14
The Nvidia performance properties sheet

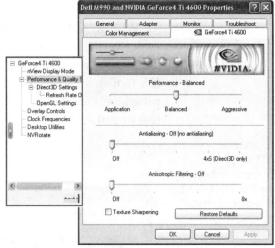

Figure 3-15
The Nvidia OpenGL
properties sheet

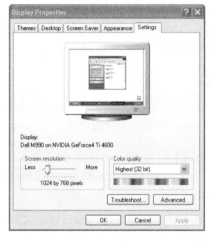

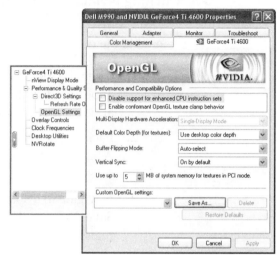

Overclocking a Graphics Card

Why settle for standard settings when you can push your graphics card to new heights? Overclocking a graphics card is easier than overclocking a processor. You can do it through Windows and see your results immediately without having to reboot constantly.

Cooling is just as big an issue for overclocked graphics cards as it is for processors. Some cards come with beefed-up coolers practically begging you to overclock them, and others come with stock coolers. If you really want to push your card to its limits and you're encountering resistance, check out card coolers at *www.frozencpu.com* or *www.2cooltek.com*.

As we said before, overclocking is a risky business. You can prematurely age and even damage your equipment. Overclock at your own risk! The philosophy behind overclocking a graphics card is the same as that of overclocking a CPU: bump up the clock speed in small increments, test for stability by running something like 3DMark2001 SE, and repeat. With graphics cards, you can often overclock the core chipset and the memory separately. That's the case with the Nvidia GeForce4 Ti series and ATI's Radeon 9500/9700 chipsets. First, increase one by 5 to 10MHz, test for stability, and then increase the other; then test for stability, and so on.

When you push too hard, you'll encounter graphical glitches, flashing textures, crashes, reboots, or other problems. Go back into the overclocking utility and back off the settings until your system is stable.

Overclocking Nvidia-Based Cards

Nvidia drivers allow you to overclock Nvidia-based cards, but you have to enable the option. To do so, you'll have to edit your registry.

1. Open the registry editor by clicking the Start menu and choosing Run. Type **regedit** into the text box and press ENTER. The registry editor will appear on your screen.

2. Back up the registry before you do anything else. Choose File | Export. A Save dialog appears. At the bottom of the dialog, click All where it says Export Range.

3. Navigate to a spot on your hard drive that you'll remember, and click Save. You now have a backup to restore in case you mess up your registry and cause something not to work.

4. Assuming you're running the latest Nvidia reference drivers, the registry editor works much like Windows Explorer. In the left pane, expand *HKEY_LOCAL_MACHINE* by clicking the tiny plus sign next to it.

5. Expand *SOFTWARE,* then *NVIDIA Corporation*, and finally *Global*. Click *NVTweak* (don't expand it; just select it), and then right-click in the right pane.

6. Choose New | DWORD Value. A new entry will appear in the right pane.

7. Name it **Coolbits**.

8. Right-click Coolbits and choose Modify. In the ensuing dialog box, make sure that Hexadecimal is selected, and in the text box under Value Data, enter **7**. When you're done, the registry should look like Figure 3-16.

Figure 3-8
The Coolbits
registry DWORD
enables GeForce
overclocking.

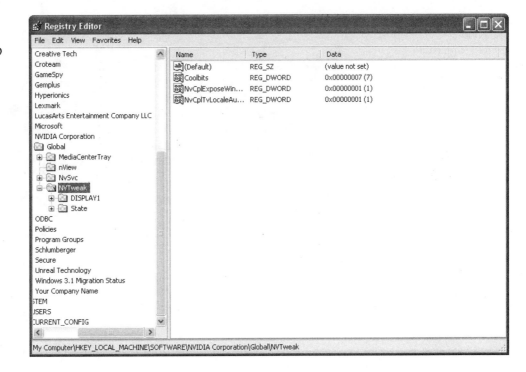

9. Click OK, exit the registry editor, and reboot the PC.

10. Now enter the Nvidia driver options shown earlier. You'll notice a new category labeled Clock Frequencies. Select it to see the overclocking page shown in Figure 3-17.

11. Check the box at the top of the page to overclock the card. The rest of the overclocking page consists of two sliders: one for the core chipset and the other for the memory. Although a button allows you to test the settings, you should run something more stringent like a current 3-D game or the old standby, 3DMark2001 SE.

Figure 3-17
The Nvidia
overclocking page

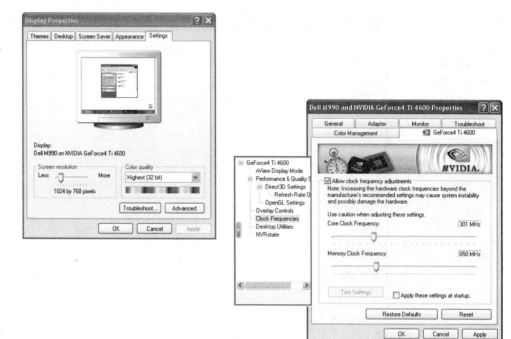

Overclocking ATI-Based Cards with PowerStrip

ATI's drivers don't have a convenient hidden overclocking tool like Nvidia's drivers. Instead, you'll have to use an application such as the wonderful PowerStrip (Figure 3-18) to help you overclock the card. A 30-day trialware version of PowerStrip can be downloaded at *www.entechtaiwan.com/ps.htm*.

Figure 3-18
PowerStrip version
3.30 is a handy video
tweaking tool.

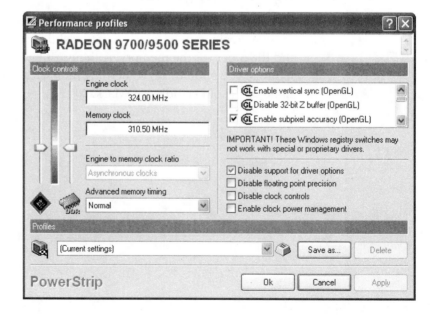

1. Download and install PowerStrip. Once it's installed, you can invoke it by right-clicking its icon in the systray (the area at the bottom right side of the Windows screen that shows the time and icons for programs running in the background) to open a menu with several options; choose Performance Profiles | Configure.

2. The resulting screen contains two sliders on its left side. Next to them is the current clock frequency of both the core chipset and the memory. Note that it shows DDR memory at its native clock frequency, not its doubled, effective frequency. To overclock the card, simply manipulate the sliders and then click Apply.

You've built up a killer system so far. You have a state-of-the-art motherboard, a speed demon of a processor, lightning memory, and a monstrous gaming graphics card. Now that your eyes have something to feast upon, it's time to treat your ears. Next up: the sound card and speakers.

Chapter 4

The Sound Card and Speakers

Tools of the Trade

A Philips head screw driver

Y ou've put together quite a system so far! With the addition of a powerful graphics card, it's ready to run the latest games at blazingly high frame rates with the detail levels turned up. Visualization is only part of the gaming experience, however; another important factor is sound.

Some game developers put a lot of work into aural immersion. Using 3-D sound APIs, they design their games to envelop players in a tapestry of aural bliss. In 3-D worlds, sounds can come from all around you, warning you of monsters attacking from behind or nefarious activity to your left or right.

To get the most out of your games, you'll need a current sound card and a set of speakers. Sound cards vary in 3-D capabilities depending on their chipsets. The best sound cards support 3-D APIs in hardware, doing the work of calculating audio signals and taking the load off the CPU. Gamers' speaker systems, meanwhile, come with various numbers of satellite speakers from two to four to five. Seven-satellite speaker systems are on the way. They also come with a subwoofer to add a solid floor of bass. Cranked up, the best speaker systems can shake the walls!

Sound cards offer other capabilities, too. They offer things like MP3 acceleration, wavetable MIDI (Musical Instrument Digital Interface) support, game ports for joysticks, gamepads and driving wheels, digital ports for speaker systems or home stereo systems, and other goodies.

Like graphics cards, sound cards are based on a chipset either made by the sound card manufacturer or licensed from another party. The chipset determines the sound card's capabilities and features. Virtually all current sound cards are compatible with Microsoft's DirectX audio APIs, DirectSound, and DirectSound3-D, but other APIs and enhancements are available. A typical sound card is shown in Figure 4-1.

Figure 4-I
A typical sound card

3-D Audio

Most 3-D games use one form or another of 3-D audio to immerse you in sound that seems to come from all directions. This can be accomplished even with only two speakers or a pair of headphones; however, in such a setup, no sound will be coming from behind you, above you, or below you—audio sources can amplify sound to appear as though it's coming from every direction.

Such 3-D audio is often accomplished with *HRTFs*, or *Head Related Transfer Functions*. The shape of your ear helps you determine the distance and location of sound sources in real life. For example, when the cordless phone starts ringing and you don't know where you left it, you can follow the sound of the ringing to locate it. Thanks to the shape of your ears, you can judge its direction and distance with only two ears; you don't need four or six ears. By the same token, you don't need more than two speakers to hear sounds from all around you when programmers use HRTFs to trick your ears into thinking the sound comes from behind, above, or below you.

Having four or more speakers does help. With an HRTF solution, if you move your head out of the "sweet spot," or if you turn your head, the illusion fades.

With speakers all around you, you can sit any way you please, turn your head, and still hear directional sound.

Another aspect of 3-D sound is *environmental* audio that uses *reverberations*. An environmental sound scheme takes into account the size and type of the room your gaming avatar is in at any given time, and it applies algorithms to the audio calculations to re-create the acoustics of each in-game room. This adds greatly to the immersion during a game—when you're in a big stone hall, sounds echo around you; when you're in a tight, claustrophobic corridor, sounds are short and snappy. The following illustration shows direct and reverberated sounds.

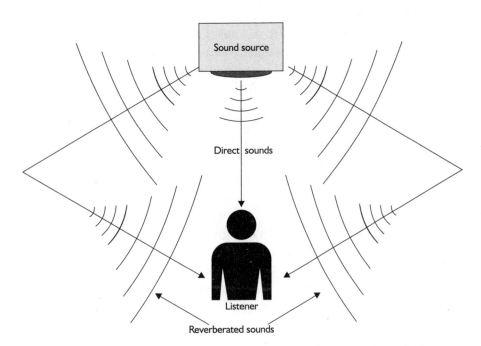

APIs and Extensions

The 3-D audio industry is mired in a soupy mix of APIs, some of which compliment each other and many that compete with each other. Some require specific audio programming in games to make them work, while others need certain hardware for full functionality. Few across-the-board standards keep everything compatible. Games with built-in 3-D audio acceleration often drop software to handle their 3-D audio needs, putting a strain on the processor and lowering in-game frame rates.

DirectSound3D

DirectSound3D (DX3D), currently referred to as Direct Audio, is part of Microsoft's DirectX suite of APIs. Providing the base level of 3-D sound support, DX3D is complimented by other APIs and extensions such as EAX. All current sound cards support Direct Audio.

Direct Audio captures audio streams from games. The streams are normally accelerated in hardware. Direct Audio is often complimented by other standards, as discussed next.

EAX 1.0 and 2.0

Written by Creative Labs, EAX (which stands for Environmental Audio eXtensions) provides audio features above what Direct Audio has to offer.

The original version of EAX features reverb effects. Direct sound is sound that you hear directly from the source; reverb is sound from the same source that bounces off of walls, pillars, and other obstacles before it reaches your ears. Reverb offers a greater level of realism than "vanilla" sound, because, of course, sound in the real world is always bouncing off obstacles. Game developers who use the EAX reverb engine don't worry about tracing every sound individually; instead, they set characteristics for rooms and other environments within their game to adjust how sounds will be heard.

EAX 2.0 offers support for occlusion and obstruction. Occlusion is the result of sounds heard through walls. For example, a sound coming from inside a wooden shack sounds quite different from a sound heard directly. Similarly, obstruction is just what it sounds like: it refers to sounds heard from behind something—for example, when there's a big rock between you and the source of the sound.

EAX Advanced HD

This recent set of extensions includes everything in earlier EAX revisions, plus a variety of new features that add realism to gaming environments. The only hardware that currently supports EAX Advanced HD is Creative Lab's SoundBlaster Audigy and Audigy 2 lines. EAX Advanced HD is the finest sounding 3-D audio API on the market. Its features are discussed in the following sections.

Multi-Environment Rendering

EAX Advanced HD can render multiple environments simultaneously. It can, for example, re-create four environments at once. Imagine a gaming environment in which you're in a small room with concrete walls and two doorways, one that leads to a huge cathedral and another that leads to a narrow corridor. EAX Advanced HD makes sure that the sounds coming from the environments through those doorways each sound the way they should (the way they would in the real world) when they reach your ears in the concrete room.

Environment Filtering

This effect is designed to help you determine the distance between you and an object making noise. It works by passing the sound data through a filter to create a noticeable effect—as you close in on the sound, it gets louder and is more detailed.

Environment Morphing

Environment morphing provides for smooth transitions of sound from one environment to another. When you pass through our theoretic doorway from the concrete room and into the cathedral, the sound changes smoothly and normally instead of snapping from one reverb effect to another.

Environment Panning

Especially effective with four-way or greater speaker setups, this feature lets you hear the sound of, say, a troll roaring in a distant cave with the cave's distance and acoustic properties preserved. If you slowly turn around your in-game character, the sound will pan smoothly from speaker to speaker. It works well in conjunction with multi-environment sounds.

Environment Reflections

This refers to the early reflections or echoes of sounds within a game environment. The echoes themselves can be panned about in 3-D. Imagine the sound of a roaring dragon in a gigantic cave. When the dragon roars, it sends out sound in all directions. The echoes come from the floor, the walls, the ceiling, and objects within the cave. As you turn or move, the echoes reach your ears realistically.

A3D 1.0 and 2.0

Now a relic of a defunct company, A3D was a terrific positional sound API that used *wave tracing* to follow the sources of sounds within games. It would then use HRTFs to re-create the positions for the user's ears. The result: with only two speakers, sounds could appear to come from anywhere around you.

Aureal, the company behind A3D and the Vortex chipsets that used it, is no longer in business; it was absorbed by Creative Labs.

Many games offered support for the A3D APIs. One of the foremost was LucasArt's *Jedi Knight*. Others, such as *Quake 2* and *Quake 3 Arena*, used A3D code within the games themselves.

Sensaura

Sensaura 3-D audio technology includes a wide variety of effects. Sensaura licenses its technology to 3-D chip makers as a plug-in for products that support its technologies. An extension of Direct Audio, its environmental subset responds to EAX calls. Most of Sensaura's effects use HRTFs to calculate the proper positioning of sounds. Sensaura's 3DPA (3-D Positional Audio) includes several subsets.

Sensaura's EnvironmentFX creates a realistic soundscape by modeling the characteristics of the room and applying algorithms to create realistic early reflections, refractions, echoes, and other effects. It takes into account the distance from the sound source, the level of direct sound from the source that reaches the user's ears, and other aspects such as objects between the user and the source and objects through which sounds can pass.

ZoomFX takes into account that not all sounds come from the same-sized source. Sounds can come from small sources, such as laughter from someone's mouth, or it can come from large, wide sources like the cheering crowd in a stadium. ZoomFX allows the size of the sound source to be set by a game's programmers.

MacroFX allows sounds from sources close to a user's head to be created accurately. Ideally, MacroFX causes audio from speakers to sound like it's within 3 feet of a user's head. Usually, close-up sounds are much louder in one ear than the other—imagine a mosquito buzzing around your right ear; you don't hear it with your left ear.

Sensaura also employs an interesting feature called VirtualEar. HRTFs depend on an "average-sized" human head. Therefore, their effectiveness depends greatly on the user's head, ear shape, and positioning. VirtualEar lets users of Sensaura licensing equipment adjust the sound to tailor it to their individual characteristics.

Sound cards that license Sensaura technology include those from Voyetra Turtle Beach, Guillemot, and VideoLogic. Audio chipsets that use Sensaura include those manufactured by ESS, Nvidia, Analog Devices, and Cirrus Logic.

QSound

Like Sensaura, QSound Labs offers a wide variety of 3-D audio APIs and extensions that can be licensed by hardware and software developers. Used by Philips in its Edge line of audio cards, QSound's various technologies act as extensions to Direct Audio, enhancing it through their own algorithms.

Q3D is the chief positional product in the lineup. Designed for both professional audio recording and computer and video gaming, Q3D includes Q1, which is used for replicating 3-D sounds from satellite speakers, and Q2, which creates 3-D sounds through a set of headphones. It does this using HRTFs.

Part of Q3D is QEM, QSound's environment modeling technology. Based on reverb, QEM applies algorithms to sound signals to give them a feeling of authenticity based on the in-game environment.

QXpander is a spatialization technology that pipes a stereo signal through an algorithm to create a wider, more enveloping sound field. It attempts to make a 2-D stereo sound appear to be 3-D, bursting out of the speakers and enveloping the listener.

QSurround reproduces multichannel audio signals to any speaker system. For example, it realistically takes a 5.1 Dolby Digital sound and faithfully reproduces it through only two speakers. It also enhances sound coming from multiple speakers, such as Dolby 4.1 and 5.1.

Audio Chipsets

The PC audio industry is similar to the graphics industry. Some card makers make their own chipsets, and others license chipsets from other companies. The audio market is messier than the graphics market, because there are more chipsets, more APIs, and just as many final market card manufacturers. To put it simply, it's a confusing mess. Following are the major audio chipsets you'll encounter.

EMU10K1

Creative Labs made the EMU10K1 audio chip for its SoundBlaster Live! series, which includes the SoundBlaster Live! and the Live! 5.1 lines. It includes 3-D acceleration of Direct Audio and one audio stream of EAX environmental audio. Figure 4-2 shows the EMU10K1.

Figure 4-2
The EMU10K1 on a
SoundBlaster Live!

Figure 4-2
The EMU10K1 on a
SoundBlaster Live!

EMU10K2

The central processor of Creative Labs' Audigy line, the EMU10K2 (Figure 4-3) was the most powerful chip of its kind until the Audigy 2 came out. The EMU10K2 introduced 24-bit audio quality, a much higher fidelity than the de facto 16-bit.

Figure 4-3
The EMU10K2 on a
SoundBlaster Audigy

CA0102

A revision of the EMU10K2, the CA0102 chip powers Creative Labs' current flagship: the Audigy 2. A powerful chip, it features Dolby Digital 6.1 decoding; 64 hardware Direct Audio voices; EAX 1.0, 2.0, and Advanced HD; and a wealth of other features. It also features the best signal-to-noise ratio available, at 106dB. The signal-to-noise ratio determines the amount of hiss you hear; the higher the number, the less hiss. The SoundBlaster Audigy 2 plays games *loud* with no noticeable hiss. This revision of the EMU10K2 is the best audio chip on the market, and we heartily recommend the Audigy 2 as part of a killer gaming system. It's shown in Figure 4-4.

Figure 4-4
The CA0102
updated EMU10K2
on a SoundBlaster
Audigy 2

Thunderbird and Thunderbird Avenger

Engineered by Philips and employed by its Edge series of sound cards, the Thunderbird line is heavily commendable. The better of the two, the Thunderbird Avenger (Figure 4-5), is found on Philips' outstanding Acoustic Edge, which is second in quality to the SoundBlaster Audigy series. Its coolest trick is its ability, through the use of QSurround, to convert stereo music to a 5.1 signal, enveloping the user in a rich audio tapestry. It supports the QSound library of APIs as well as EAX 1.0 and 2.0.

Figure 4-5
The Thunderbird
Avenger chip on
Philips' Acoustic
Edge

Sound Fusion CS4630

These capable chipsets are employed by cards from Hercules and Voyetra Turtle Beach. Hercules' Game Theater XP and Voyetra's Santa Cruz use the top of the line SoundFusion CS4630 (Figure 4-6), which accelerates Direct Audio and supports EAX 1.0 and 2.0. It also features S/PDIF (Sony/Philips Digital Interface) support for Dolby Digital 5.1 output to compatible speakers.

Figure 4-6
The SoundFusion
CS4630 on Hercules'
Game Theater XP

Canyon3D-2

You'll encounter the Canyon3D-2 chip on the I/O Magic Hurricane Extreme (shown in Figure 4-7). It features hardware support for 64 Direct Audio streams, EAX 1.0 and 2.0, the Sensaura family of extensions, and more. In our tests, the Hurricane Extreme utilized more CPU time than our recommended solutions and its sound wasn't as crisp.

Figure 4-7
The Canyon3D-2
on I/O Magic's
Hurricane Extreme

Motherboard Sound: Avoid It

Other audio chipsets exist, but many of these are featured on motherboards themselves (see Figure 4-8). As a general rule, motherboard audio isn't as robust or as widely compatible as the sound you can get from a good sound card. In addition, many motherboards offer only stereo-out ports for speaker support; to get 4.1 or 5.1 support, you often have to buy a separate daughter card. We recommend that you disable onboard audio through the motherboard's BIOS setup program and use a high-quality sound card instead.

Figure 4-8
Some motherboards have onboard audio; disable it.

Sound Card Characteristics

All sound cards have similar physical characteristics. Once you've dealt with one or two cards, you'll feel comfortable with any sound card on the market.

You'll find several internal ports on a sound card. They're usually black in color. Some sound cards have many ports, and some have only one. The port you'll find on any sound card is usually labeled "CD_IN." It allows you to route CD audio signals through the sound card so that they can be played on your system speakers. Most sound cards and CD/DVD-ROM drives and burners come with a round, gray cable with four wires for this purpose.

You may also see a 2-pin S/PDIF port for the same purpose. The 4-pin port is analog, and the 2-pin port is digital. It's extremely difficult to hear the difference between one and the other.

You'll find several external ports on the rear metal gate. Two ports found on all current sound cards are front and rear stereo out ports. They're in the form of 1/8-inch minijacks and are intended for four-speaker stereo systems. You'll also find a microphone-in port, to which you connect a microphone that you can use in many multiplayer games, and a line-in port for piping signals from a stereo or another source.

Most sound cards still have a 15-pin MIDI/gameport, as shown next. This can be used to connect a joystick, gamepad, driving wheel, or other game controller, or it can be used as an in/out port for MIDI instruments such as electronic keyboards.

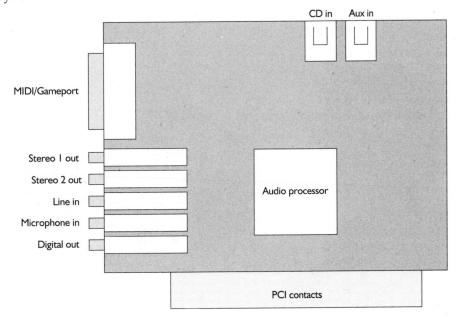

Other Features

While nearly all sound cards conform to the characteristics mentioned, many offer features above and beyond the standard set. Besides audio quality, a rich set of extra features can make or break a sound card.

Digital Out

Most current sound cards offer a S/PDIF digital port for piping digital signals to compatible speaker systems. This is a must for true Dolby Digital 5.1 or Dolby Digital EX 6.1 audio. Dolby standards are used chiefly for movies played on a system's DVD-ROM drive, but some games take advantage of them, too. Philips Acoustic Edge can take in-game, stereo music coming from the game's CD-ROM (this is known as *Redbook* audio) and expand it to a full 5.1 speaker system, while keeping the in-game positional sound effects accurate.

External Consoles

Some sound cards, such as Creative Labs' SoundBlaster Audigy Platinum and Audigy 2 platinum and Hercules' Game Theater XP, offer consoles with additional ports and controls.

Creative Labs consoles mount in a case's 5-inch external drive bay. They have microphone inputs, DIN-style MIDI ports, optical in and out ports, and other ports. Interestingly, the Audigy and Audigy 2 Platinum editions also have a remote control that can be used to start and control DVD-ROMs and music CDs, adjust the volume, and perform other common remote-control functions. This expands the sound cards' capabilities into the realm of home theaters. The external console of Audigy 2 is shown in Figure 4-9.

Figure 4-9
The external console of a SoundBlaster Audigy 2

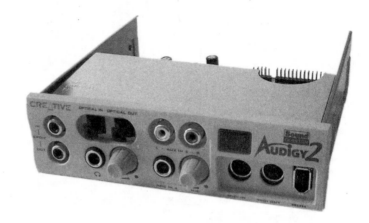

The Game Theater XP has a big external console (Figure 4-10) that must be set on the computer desk or on top of the PC. It connects to the back of the sound card and has all the audio input and output ports built into it. This makes it handy for when you're plugging in a set of speakers, because it's easier to deal with a console than to have to turn the computer around to see the audio ports. It also features a microphone port, a line-out port, and, of all things, a 4-port USB hub.

Figure 4-10
The external console of a Hercules Game Theater XP

Turtle Beach's VersaJack

Unique to Turtle Beach Santa Cruz is the VersaJack, a configurable 1/8-inch minijack that's software configurable. It performs various functions, depending on the needs of the user: it can be an analog out port for two extra speakers (the card has two stereo out ports for front and rear pairs), a stereo out port for headphones, a line-in port for rear signal input, or a digital S/PDIF port.

FireWire ports

Creative Labs has made a name for itself in the FireWire community by offering FireWire (IEEE1394) ports as part of its Audigy sound cards (see Figure 4-11). One port resides on the metal rear gate, and on Platinum editions another resides on the front console. SoundBlaster calls its ports SB1394, but they're compatible with any IEEE1394 device. Hercules' recent DigiFire 7.1 sound card includes a pair of FireWire ports on its rear gate.

Figure 4-11
The Audigy 2 has a FireWire port on its rear panel.

Choosing a Sound Card

Dozens of sound cards are available, with all kinds of different features. Based on their audio quality and feature sets, we recommend three cards: Creative Labs SoundBlaster Audigy 2, Hercules DigiFire 7.1, and Philips Acoustic Edge.

Creative Labs' SoundBlaster Audigy 2

Creative Labs' SoundBlaster Audigy 2 is, hands-down, the best sounding audio card for the money. The Audigy 2 doesn't feature the console that the Platinum edition does, but it has everything a gamer needs for an aurally immersive gaming experience. Feature rich, it has a FireWire port, 6.1 speaker support, and a Dolby Digital EX decoder. The Audigy cards are the only products that support the incredible EAX Advanced HD. And to top it all off, the Audigy 2 is THX-certified, meaning it's passed stringent testing procedures put forth by LucasArts.

The Hercules DigiFire 7.1

The Hercules DigiFire 7.1 is the first 7.1 solution available, although 7.1 speaker systems are still a long way off. The DigiFire 7.1 boasts two FireWire ports, a digital out port, as well as the usual stereo out and microphone and line-in ports. It supports the Sensaura family of APIs as well as DirectSound3D, EAX 1.0, and EAX 2.0. The major downside is that its only S/PDIF support is optical; there's no coaxial jack.

Philips Acoustic Edge

This terrific sound card may be more than a year old, but it holds its own against the rest of the market. It supports DirectSound3D in hardware and QSound's family of APIs through drivers, and it has the unique capability to turn two-speaker stereo signals into rich 5.1 tapestries.

Installing a Sound Card

Installing a sound card is similar to installing a graphics card: you set the contacts into the proper expansion slot and fasten it down with a screw (see Figure 4-12).

Figure 4-12
Installing a
sound card

Caution

Be sure to be static-safe! See Chapter 2 for hints on how to handle static electricity.

1. Open your case and locate the row of PCI slots. They're usually white, but not always (see Figure 4-13). They're a series of short slots starting next to the AGP slot and continuing on across the motherboard.

2. Choose a slot, and remove the corresponding metal gate cover from the back of the PC.

Figure 4-13
PCI slots on a motherboard

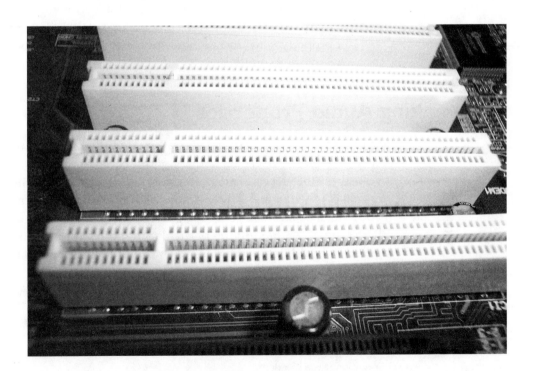

3. Slide your sound card into the slot, with the contacts down and the metal gate facing the back of the box. Figure 4-14 shows the contacts on a sound card. Make sure it's seated completely, and secure it with a screw. You're done, unless you're working with an Audigy 2.

Figure 4-14
The contacts on
a sound card

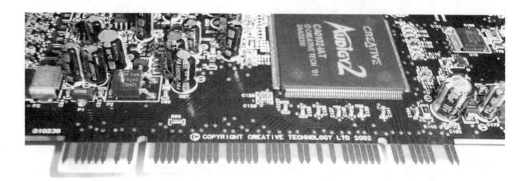

4. For the Audigy 2, you'll need to follow a few more steps. Find the box containing the front console and the pertinent cables. Follow the manufacturer's instructions on how to install the console and connect it properly. Then install the software as instructed. Note that you cannot overclock a sound card.

Tweaking Audio Properties

Sound card driver interfaces let you tailor your music and gaming experiences to suit your whims. Most come with a Control Panel program and a systray icon to invoke these interfaces. Driver interfaces all are remarkably similar, and they let you make adjustments to such things as the number of speakers you have to work with, a headphone setting, a graphic equalizer setting, balance, gain, and other settings common to the particular brand of sound card you've surfaced. Most sound card driver interfaces are similar to the SoundBlaster Audigy 2 interface shown in Figure 4-15.

Figure 4-15
The Audigy 2
mixer application

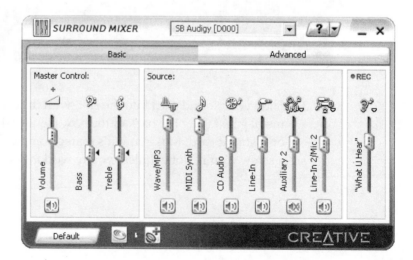

Speaker Systems

Multimedia speakers have come a long way from the cheap, unpowered placeholders that once ruled the market—or, God forbid, the internal PC speaker. Even the first powered PC speakers were subpar, with their hissing, grainy sound. Only in the past few years have they come close to the rich sound you hear in a good home stereo system. In some cases, PC speaker systems have even surpassed home theater quality.

Speaker Features

Like sound cards, speakers feature a number of options that enhance their value and make gaming life easier or more pleasurable for the user. Of course, the key ingredients in a good speaker system is the clearness, accuracy, and power of its sound, but other conveniences do make a difference. For example, when Klipsch came out with its THX-certified ProMedia v.4-200 which hailed a renaissance for PC sound. It was clear, crisp, and had in-your-face power. However, it lacked an on/off switch, a headphone jack, and other conveniences that would have enhanced it as a product. (Klipsch remedied this in its ProMedia 4.1.)

2.0, 2.1, 4.1, and 5.1

Speakers come in various configurations, and they're designated with a number, a dot, and another number, like so: 2.0. The first number indicates the number of satellite speakers the system includes. The second number indicates the number of subwoofers in the system. 2.0, 2.1, 4.1, and 5.1 setups are most common. Believe it or not, there is such a thing as 5.2 speakers with dual subwoofers. A loud base noise can blow the roof off a house.

For gaming, you'll want to concentrate on 4.1 or 5.1 speaker systems. 4.1 speaker systems usually have two audio inputs to correspond with the two audio outputs on a sound card: front stereo and rear stereo. The best 5.1 speaker systems have a digital in port of some kind, so you can pump digital 5.1 sound directly into the system for maximum clarity and convenience.

If you're severely limited in space and have nowhere to mount rear speakers, check out 2.1 systems. Don't bother with 2.0 unless you don't care for high-fidelity bass. You'll be missing out, though: there's nothing like the bass kick when you fire a shotgun in *Quake* or hear a helicopter crash in *Delta Force: Black Hawk Down*.

Conveniences

The best speaker systems feature minor conveniences such as volume, tone, and fade control on one of the front satellite speakers or on a separate console. While you can adjust the sound through the graphic equalizer component of your sound card's driver controls, it's nice to be able to lower the base with a turn of the knob when your neighbor downstairs starts pounding on his ceiling.

Another nice convenience to look for is a headphone jack, which may be positioned on a front satellite or control console. When you connect a set of headphones, equipped speaker systems will shut off their own sound. This is great for long, late-night game sessions so you can play at ear-splitting volumes without waking the baby.

Rear speaker stands come with certain speaker systems, and they're nice to have. Finding a place to mount rear speakers can be a problem, though, because not all of us have a pair of convenient tables behind our gaming rig on which to set the surround satellites. Cambridge SoundWorks speakers, from Creative Labs, often come with rear speaker tripods.

Choosing a Speaker System

We recommend two speaker systems with absolute confidence that you'll like both. We've tested dozens, and for gaming purposes the two here are stellar. They offer power, fidelity, and accuracy beyond anything else available.

Logitech's Z680 5.1 speaker system (Figure 4-16) offers a tremendous value for your money without shirking anything in terms of power or clarity. Equipped with two digital inputs and analog inputs as well, it's ready for current generation sound cards with digital-out ports.

Figure 4-16
Logitech's Z680 5.1
speaker system

Klipsch's ProMedia 5.1 is ridiculously powerful. Even at half volume it will cause your ears to ring. This speaker system is aimed squarely at gamers who want earthquake bass and brash power. Its only downside is that it lacks digital inputs; it has three analog inputs—one for front stereo, one for rear stereo, and one for center/bass.

Setting Up a Speaker System

The placement of your speakers is important to your gaming experience. Satellite speakers must be placed properly, relative to where you sit.

Ideally, the front speakers should be spaced so that their distance from each other is equal to the distance between you and their center point. Don't point them directly at where you'll be sitting; instead, point them so that they're perpendicular to your desk. See the following illustration for an idea of how your speakers should be placed.

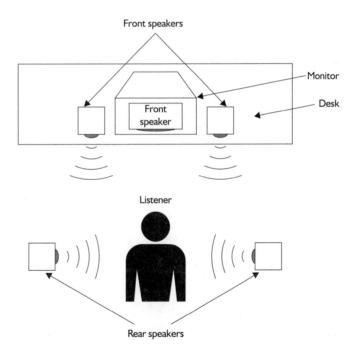

If your speaker system has a center speaker, it should be placed directly in front of you. That can be a bother with your keyboard and monitor already in front of you. Place it on top of your monitor if you can, or, if necessary, build or purchase a stand for your monitor to make space on your desk for the center speaker.

Rear speakers should point toward each other, and they should sit slightly behind your head. They should each be 3 to 5 feet away from you, and set symmetrically so that the distance from each speaker to your head is the same.

Now your sound card is installed and your speakers are in place. Before you can set up an operating system, you need a place to put it. You also need a drive to read it. The next chapter covers storage, which includes hard drives and optical drives. It also tackles a terrific way to keep cool air flowing through your case.

Chapter 5

Storage, Cooling, and Finishing Up

Tools of the Trade

A medium Philips head screwdriver

Your computer is so cool that your fingers freeze to it when you touch it. You've got killer graphics and sound, a monstrous processor, and a terrific motherboard. What's next?

Your PC handles data in main memory, but where does it put all the stuff that it's not using? Moreover, where does it get new data? The answer is *storage*, a blanket term meaning its hard disk drives, floppy drive, and optical drives. Each, save for maybe the floppy drive, is critical to a system.

Hard Drives

Here's a tried-and-true analogy. Think of an accountant with a typical office, he has a desk, a desk drawer, and a file cabinet. The stuff he works on directly on his desk may be considered the CPU. The data he plans to work on next or has just worked on goes into his desk drawer, which could be thought of as a system's memory.

He also needs a place to store all the paperwork that he's not planning to deal with right away or that he's done with for the time being. Thus, he shuffles across his office to his file cabinet and shoves it in there. The file cabinet can be thought of as the hard drive. A typical hard drive is shown in Figure 5-1.

A hard disk drive is a case with a printed circuit board (PCB) controller board. Inside the case are a number of disk shaped platters. A magnetic head moves about those platters to store and retrieve data. Unlike system memory, the magnetic data on a hard drive stays there even when you turn off the computer.

Two major factors define the performance of hard drives: *seek time* and *transfer rate*. The faster a hard drive can find the requested data the better, and the faster it can shuffle the data into memory the better also.

EIDE Vs. SCSI

There's a war going on between two types of hard drive controllers and the drives themselves. The de facto standard in the hard drive industry is ATA (Advanced Technology Attachment, which is sometimes known as IDE, for Integrated Device Electronics). Its enemy, which is far less common but wields a rabid following, is SCSI (Small Computer System Interface).

The two controllers have a number of differences that are complicated by the number of flavors of both. ATA drives come in types including ATA-33, ATA-66, ATA-100, and ATA-133. Each supports a faster burst rate than the last. Meanwhile, SCSI comes in SCSI-1, SCSI-2 (known as plain SCSI), SCSI-3, and more.

Furthermore, a new and faster type of ATA is just emerging while this book is being written. It's called Serial ATA, and it should catch on in the next few years. It's too early to tell if the gaming community will unite behind it.

Figure 5-1
A typical hard drive

Gaming benchmarks show little difference between SCSI and ATA. For the purposes of this book, we'll assume you'll be using ATA-100 or ATA-133 equipment, and here's why:

❏ *ATA is cheaper.* Not only are ATA drives less expensive than SCSI counterparts, but you also need a special PCI adapter to use them.

❏ *ATA is available on most motherboards.* Nearly all motherboards come with ATA adapters built in. ATA supports two channels for each connector on board, so there's plenty of room for a hard drive, a CD-ROM drive, and a high-capacity removable drive if you want one. Few motherboards come with SCSI onboard.

❏ *ATA is easier to use.* It's not mired in dozens of standards with tons of different connectors, capabilities, and compatabilities.

Given that ATA-100 features more speed than games actually need, there's no good reason to go with SCSI. SCSI pundits will hate this, but facts are facts.

Optical Drives

Along with a hard drive, you'll need one or more optical drives: a CD-ROM drive, DVD-ROM drive, CD-RW, DVD-RAM drive, or another type of drive. A typical CD-ROM drive is shown in Figure 5-2.

You'll need these for two purposes: All software currently available comes on CD-ROM or, rarely, DVD-ROM discs. Without an optical reader, you won't be able to install games. Second, you might want to create your own CD-ROMs. This is called *burning*, and it is useful for backing up programs that you already

Figure 5-2
A typical
CD-ROM drive

have and for creating compilations for music that you download over the Internet (non-copyrighted material, of course).

CD-ROMs and DVD-ROMs

Internal ROM (read-only memory) drives are intended to be mounted in one of your case's 5-inch external drive bays. They normally come with screws, and they sometimes come with a round audio cable, as discussed in Chapter 4.

CD-ROM readers come in two major types: CD-ROM drives and DVD-ROM drives. The former read only CDs, while the latter read DVD-ROMs and movie DVDs; they often come with software MPEG-2 decoders so you can enjoy DVD films on your PC. Popular decoders are PowerDVD and WinDVD. DVD-ROM drives also feature graphical front ends to let you play, pause, fast-forward, rewind, and watch frame by frame.

Note that neither CD-ROM drives nor DVD-ROM drives write data to disks. For that, you'll need a CD-RW or DVD-RW/RAM disc. These are commonly called *burners*.

Burners

CD-RW (CD-rewritable) burners can be used for a variety of purposes, from backing up data to creating music CDs from MP3 files. Bundled with burning software, they can also be used to copy CD-ROMs. This process goes even more quickly when you have a CD or DVD-ROM reader in which to put the source disc, and your CD-RW, in which to put the black CD (or destination disc).

Newer to the mix is DVD burning equipment. With it, you can, for example, take your own home video and burn it to DVD discs that are playable on nearly every DVD player out there.

What to Buy

Choosing storage is a daunting task, with dozens of hard drives available, and scads of CD and DVD readers and writers. Walk down the shelves of your local computer shop and you'll end up with more questions than you had before you entered the store.

Choose a hard drive by *spin rate*, which is the speed in rotations per minute (RPMs), capacity, and brand. Note that benchmarks show little difference between ATA-100 and ATA-133 drives. Save your money and get an ATA-100.

We suggest two optical drives if you can afford them. One should be a DVD-ROM drive, for reading both CDs and DVDs. The other should be a burner of some type. This not only copy disks quickly, but it also leaves you ready in case games ever make the transition from CD-ROMs to DVD-ROMs. Plus, you can watch movies on your PC, and with your killer sound system it could be a heck of an experience. Our favorite brand of CD-ROM and DVD-ROM drives is Toshiba.

Installing a Hard Drive

Most computer cases have removable 3-inch drive bays (shown in Figure 5-3). You'll want to remove yours before you proceed.

1. Make sure your hard drive is the "master" or "only" drive. Check the sticker on the top of the drive, which will feature a diagram of a pin configuration and show you where a jumper should go for each of its various configurations. Then look on the back of the drive and ensure that the jumper is either in the master configuration, or, if there's one available, the solo configuration. Figure 5-4 shows the jumpers.

2. Slide the drive into one of the bays. It should sit so that the rear half of the drive sticks out. Line up the screw holes and insert one screw. Don't tighten it all the way. Do the same until you have four screws loosely seated. Then go around and tighten them all up.

Figure 5-3
A removable
drive bay

Figure 5-4
Setting the jumpers

3. Now find the ribbon cable that came with your motherboard. One end might be blue. Locate the primary IDE port, labeled either "IDE0" or "IDE1," on the motherboard. Install the cable carefully. Then insert the other end of the cable into the 40-pin connector on your hard drive. See Figure 5-5.

Figure 5-5
Installing the
ribbon cable

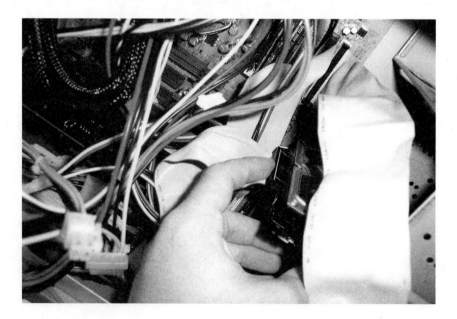

Creator: Steve Rawczak
Case: MaverikV

Creator: Bill McBride
Case: Blue Azure
www.c3case.com

Creator: Chris Christman

Creator: Kyle Blair

Creator: Jani Ponkko
www.metku.net

Creator: Ed Chen
Case: Red Marble
www.gideontech.com

Creator: Jeremy Melton
Case: Biohazard

Creator: Jeremy Melton
Case: Biohazard

Creator: Luke Hachmeister
Case: Insight
www.merliniworks.com

Creator: Luke Hachmeister
Case: Impulse
www.merliniworks.com

Creator: Sam Beck
Case: Tantric

Creator: Kile Lindgren
Case: Plexi

Note that ribbon cables come with one pink ribbon to the side. This corresponds with the pin numbered "1" on the motherboard and usually faces the power supply connector on the hard drive. Most cables are designed so that you cannot put them in backward. If the cable doesn't slide in, don't use excessive force!

4. Now find a four-wire Molex connector hanging from your power supply. Connect it to the 4-pin receptacle on your hard drive, as shown in Figure 5-6.

5. Slide the 3-inch drive bay back into place. If all went well, your hard drive should be installed. You can check and see how it went if you have a monitor handy.

6. Plug AC into the monitor and the computer, and connect the monitor's data cable to your video card. Fire up the computer. The POST screen should automatically detect the hard drive (Figure 5-7). If it does not, turn off and unplug the computer. Make sure all the cables are seated properly and that the power connector is firmly seated in the hard drive.

Installing Optical Drives

Installing optical drives is similar to installing a hard drive.

1. First, you have to remove the front bezels from your computer where you want your drives to go. You may have to break out a metal plate.

Figure 5-6
Connecting the power cable

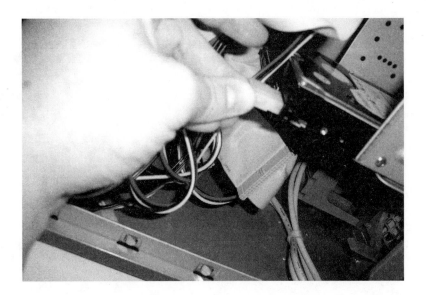

Figure 5-7
The POST routine
will detect a properly
installed hard drive.

2. Take the second IDE cable from your motherboard's collection. Install
   one side into the second IDE connector, and work it through to the top
   of the case. See Figure 5-8. It should have two connectors on it; use one
   for one optical drive and the other for the second optical drive.

Figure 5-8
Installing the
IDE cable

Figure 5-9
Setting optical
drive jumpers

3. Look at the top of the drives for master/slave designations. Using the jumpers on the back of the drives (Figure 5-9), make one a master and the other a slave. Then insert the drives into their bays. Connect power and ribbon cables.

4. Choose the drive through which you plan to listen to CD music and connect the two- or four-ribbon audio cable. Make sure the cable is also connected to the CD-in port on your sound card. Then, slide the drive into place, as shown in Figure 5-10.

Figure 5-10
Installing the
optical drives

5. Screw the drives into place. Then perform the POST test as described in step 6 of the hard-drive section. The POST screen should detect each drive, as shown in Figure 5-11.

Cooling

Proper air cooling is essential for keeping your computer running smoothly. Cooling will require fans above and beyond the exhaust fan blowing out the back of your power supply.

You'll want a second exhaust fan mounted on the rear of the box. Check the specs of your computer's case to see what size fan you need; they range from 80mm up to 120mm. The exhaust fan will draw air into the box through ambient holes.

Figure 5-11
The POST screen should reflect the presence of the optical drives.

You should also consider mounting one or two 80mm fans on the front of the box, drawing air inward. Intake fans require filters to keep them from sucking dust into the case. Fans and filters are available at sites such as *www.coolerguys.com* or *www.frozencpu.com*.

Set up an airflow system like the one shown in the following diagram.

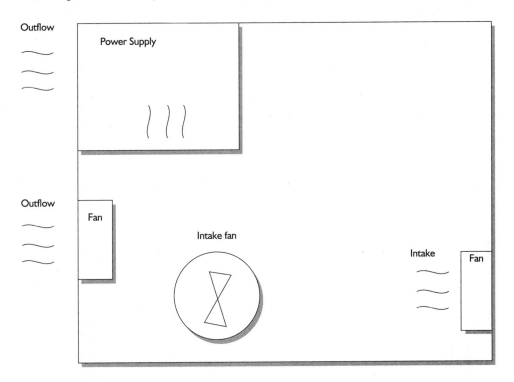

You might also consider installing side fans to cool your cards. Some cases already have holes in their sides for fans. If not, you'll have to create your own blow holes, as covered in Chapter 7.

Chapter 6
Outside the Box

Tools of the Trade

Just your fingers

Y ou've built up a darn near perfect system, complete with a modern CPU, speedy RAM, a super-efficient motherboard, a titan of a graphics card, and a sound system that can destroy small buildings. There's more to go, however. A superior gaming system has external needs as well as internal ones. You need a great keyboard, a responsive mouse, and maybe a joystick or driving controller.

Of course, you want the best that's out there. However, unlike internal components, no benchmarks are available to set one keyboard or joystick apart from another. Controller quality is a highly subjective issue. In this section, we'll list our favorite ones, but you may find different products that you prefer.

Try Them Out

Most computer stores have joysticks and mice on display that you can actually touch and use. Visit those aisles to see what fits your hand the best and what feels right for you.

The Monitor

Flat-panel monitors are all the rage, but they're not the best option for gamers. For one thing, a high-quality flat panel costs much more than its *CRT* (*cathode ray tube*) counterpart. Another problem is refresh rate: flat-panel monitors have lower refresh rates than CRT monitors, limiting the frame rate at which you can play games.

Monitor sizes are measured diagonally. For example, a 19-inch monitor with 18-inch viewable screen would measure 18 inches from one corner to the diagonal corner. It's important to distinguish between the size of the view screen and the viewable area, because part of the view screen is covered by the monitor's bezel.

There's a difference between a flat-screen CRT monitor and a flat-panel monitor. You'll want a big flat-screen CRT monitor.

The Keyboard

A great deal of first-person shooters are controlled with a keyboard and/or mouse. That's why it's important to get a keyboard with excellent tactile response that generally feels good.

Among the dozens of keyboards, two stand out. For a budget price, the Key Tronic (Figure 6-1) has terrific response and nice big keys, and it's very reliable; I've had one for more than six years and it still works perfectly.

Figure 6-1
This classic, no-frills Key Tronic keyboard has the right feel for gaming.

The other favorite is Microsoft's Internet Keyboard. This keyboard is a little mushier than the Key Tronic, but it features functionality above and beyond your standard QWERTY keyboard.

The Microsoft Internet Keyboard also features shortcut keys to open a browser, search the Internet, open e-mail, and perform other mundane but common tasks.

The Mouse

Just as important in first-person shooters as the keyboard, a mouse must be comfy, feature lots of buttons, have a scroll wheel, and be accurate.

Mice work by tracking the motion of the mouse relative to the surface it's on. Until recently, mice used balls on their undersides to track motion. This caused problems: when the ball got dirty or the internal rotors became dusty, the mouse wouldn't operate properly.

That's why we recommend an LED-based optical mouse. These mice use a light sensor and receiver to track their motion. They can't get dirty, as the sensor and the light are recessed. You should use a good-sized mouse pad with your optical mouse to prevent cursor skips and jumps.

At this particular time, *the* mouse to have is a Logitech MX 500, or, for a cordless version, the 700 is a gem. The MX 500 is versatile, with many programmable buttons, a scroll wheel (usually used in games to select weapons), and a smooth, comfortable surface. Relatively new, it features more accurate tracking technology than most optical mice. Figure 6-2 shows Logitech's MX 500.

Figure 6-2
The Logitech MX 500 mouse is full of extra buttons and is comfortable to boot.

Personalize Your Mouse

You can program the mouse buttons to use during game play. Simply use the mouse interface to program the buttons to F-keys (the function keys along the top of your keyboard), allowing your game program to use the F-keys as you please. For example, you can program the side button (on the mouse) to F2, and in the game make F2 your "jump" key. When you press the side button in a game, your character will jump.

Game Controllers

Along with mice and keyboards, some games benefit greatly from specialized game controllers. For example, sports games are best played with gamepads, while flight sims absolutely require a good joystick or a flight control system.

The vast majority of game controllers are USB parts, so you don't have to worry about the gameport on the back of your sound card. Furthermore, all game controllers come with profiling software that lets you program keys, or sets of keys, to certain buttons. This is great for creating one-click combos in fighting games (if you can find one for the PC).

Joysticks

You'll find dozens of joysticks available for the PC, even though the most popular games are controlled with the keyboard and/or mouse. Two types of joysticks are available: those with, and those without, *force feedback*. Used well by developers, force feedback can enhance the immersion experience while you're playing a game. They can replicate the subtle forces of wind sheer or the pings of your plane getting riddled with bullets. Poor force-feedback programming can go from an immersive-plus to a jerky, jolting experience that makes control more difficult and deters from the realism of a game.

A food force feedback joystick, Microsoft's SideWinder Force Feedback 2 is a comfortable joystick with a twist "z" axis, a throttle wheel, and plenty of programmable buttons. Its forces range from feather light to downright jolting.

For flight sim fanatics, the shining star of a product is the X45 system from Saitek (Figure 6-3). It features both a joystick and throttle unit, each of which is encrusted with more buttons than jewels on a crown. Though it's complex to learn, if flight sims are your bag it's easily the best control system out there.

Figure 6-3
Saitek's X45 is a full-featured flight control system.

Driving Wheels

If you haven't played a racing game with a driving wheel, you haven't really played a racing game—controlling them with a joystick just isn't natural. You'll need a good wheel with a solid clamping system and good force feedback, as most racing games benefit from force feedback. In case you don't care for force feedback, most games let you turn it off and the motors in the wheel create a virtual center and appropriate tension. You also need a heavy pedal system that won't slide around under your feet.

Logitech's MOMO racing wheel (Figure 6-4) delivers the goods with gusto. As *the* racing wheel to own, it's so popular that it's often sold out. If you have to put one on back order, it's worth the wait; anything else is an inferior product.

Figure 6-4
Logitech's MOMO force-feedback wheel is outstanding.

Gamepads

Used mainly for sports and arcade games, gamepads aren't as prevalent for the PC as they are for consoles. They do have their place, though, and it's handy to have one when you need one. Current gamepads have a directional D-pad, two analog thumb controllers, and a slew of buttons and triggers, which can usually be programmed in the same manner in which joysticks are programmed.

Logitech's Rumblepad (Figure 6-5) has a satisfyingly jittery force feedback, with discreet left and right motors. It comes in two versions: corded and cordless. The cordless is great because you don't have to worry about the cord getting wound up in all your stuff, but it does require frequent battery replacement.

Figure 6-5
This cordless
WingMan Rumblepad
is terrific for
arcade-style games.

Multiplayer Gaming

Whether you've got a cable modem, a DSL (digital subscriber line) Internet connection, a dial-up connection, or just a stand-alone system, one of the most compelling aspects of gaming is playing with other human beings. This can be done through online gaming or through setting up a *LAN*, or Local Area Network, which is a framework of multiple connected computers.

Online Gaming

For online gaming, *ping* is king. Ping is the amount of time that it takes for data to reach another system, whether it be online or in a LAN, and return to your computer. The higher the ping, the more *latency* you're dealing with. Latency is detrimental to online gaming; it can cause skips, interfere with aiming, and cause other problems depending on how the game itself deals with latency.

Server browsers usually show your ping time to each server on their list. Some games, such as *Quake 3 Arena, Counter Strike,* and *Unreal Tournament 2003,* have built-in server browsers that go out and look for servers on which you can play. Other games, like *GameSpy Arcade,* rely on third-party server browsers. Regardless, you'll want to join a game that has the lowest ping possible. This will ensure smooth multiplayer gaming, much like a high-frame rate ensures smooth animation. Using a broadband Internet connection, such as a cable modem or a DSL service, provides superior ping times compared with a slower dial-up connection.

LAN Gaming

Another way to reduce latency to almost zero is to invite some friends to bring their PCs over and have a LAN party. To set up a LAN, you'll need a hub (preferably a 10/100 auto-sensing hub), and each player will need an Ethernet adapter in his or her computer. You'll also need CAT5 cables for each computer.

An alternative to that is wireless networking, in which a wireless access point takes place of the hub, and each computer needs a wireless network adapter. No cables are needed for wireless networking. Currently, two standards of wireless networks exist: 802.11b, the most prevalent standard, and 802.11a, a faster emerging standard. 802.11b is fine for gaming purposes.

Windows XP's networking wizard takes care of most of the grunt work of networking. It will automatically detect that you have an adapter in your computer and ask for drivers if necessary. Run the network setup wizard. Make sure that when you choose a workgroup name, everybody chooses the same name (make it something easy, like WORKGROUP).

Windows installs *TCP/IP (Transmission Control Protocol/Internet Protocol)* automatically. Most current games use TCP/IP to communicate over a network. Some older games use *IPX/SPX (Internetwork Packet Exchange/Sequenced Packet Exchange),* so you may want to install that, too. Here's how to do so:

1. Open the Control Panel.

2. Open Network Connections.

3. Go to Local Area Network. A properties sheet will appear.

4. Click the Properties button. Another sheet will appear.

5. Click the Install button.

6. Double-click NWLink IPX/SPX/Netbios Compatible Transport Protocol.

7. Click OK. You'll be asked to reboot the computer.

When your computers are networked, all you have to do is have one person start the game and choose to host a session. Other players on the LAN may then start the game and look for a LAN session.

Now that you've built the perfect PC, it's time to make it yours. Modding your system is a way of putting your unique mark on it, making it something to look at, making it cool, making it *yours*. The next three chapters will cover modding in detail.

Part II

Modding the Case

Chapter 7

Window
Construction

Tools of the Trade

Rotary tool or jig saw

Drill with various-sized bits

Scrap paper or newspaper

Hobby knife

Screwdriver

Sandpaper

Acrylic sheet

Velcro, nuts and bolts, rubber molding, or rivets to secure the window

80, 92, or 120mm case fan

Fan grill

Fan screws

Before starting this project, some basic tools and techniques need to be discussed. The main focus here will be the use of power tools, which can cost from $50 to $100 and more, depending on brand and model. You can pick up most of the tools you need at any hardware store; often you'll choose from among a wide selection of tools in the power tool aisle. You can purchase the items recommended here or go with any of the various brands and models. Most of the tools you need may already be in your garage or workshop. This list is not the only possible way to create a window; it is just a starting point to guide you in the right direction.

TIPS OF
THE TRADE

Choosing the Right Equipment

Not all tools are created equal—as with buying an automobile, it is best to test them out at the store if you can, before you buy. Get a feel for the weight and grip, and choose the one that best suits your needs.

Introduction to Window Construction

The preceding chapters explained how to build and configure the ultimate high-performance personal computer. With so much firepower sitting inside a case, it would be a shame to keep it bottled up. You can add more spice to the tower in a number of ways. In the chapters that follow, you'll read about some simple projects that will add new and exciting elements to your tower case.

Let's start with the easiest and probably the most noticeable modification: the case window. Nearly all stock cases follow the same design and have the similar beige color. With so many advanced PC users, a change in the norm was much needed. Cutting out a window in the case is not at all a new art form; many of you may have already used or witnessed it in the car stereo market. Clear acrylic windows protect amplifiers and other car stereo components in the trunk, while letting people view what's on the inside. The case window is no different; it allows you to see the inside of the box, as shown in Figure 7-1.

Figure 7-1
A case window

Some component manufacturers sell colored parts, such as red motherboards and video cards. These colorful components would be pointless inside a regular case, since you could not see them. Having a window is the best way to showcase the actual hardware that is installed in your system. While the most obvious place for a window is on the side panel of a case, you can install other accessories to enhance the overall look of your PC tower—including top case windows and clever ways of securing them to your case.

Creating a case window requires the right tools as well as the right methods. The most important rule while working on your creation is safety. Because you're using power tools to cut metal and acrylic, you need to follow appropriate precautions to keep yourself safe. Safety goggles, as well as gloves, are highly recommended. A large, clean, and well-lit work area is definitely necessary. If you're cutting plastic, it's best done outside or in a well-ventilated area, since melting plastic should not be inhaled.

The best cutting tool to use on the case is a matter of contention. Many prefer the slower precision cutting that a rotary tool can provide, while others appreciate the speed of a jig saw. To clear up this confusion before starting, you should think of the ideal cutting device as the tool you are most comfortable with and can afford. A jig saw may cost hundreds of dollars, for example, while a rotary tool might set you back about $50. Spending lots of money on a tool you will use only once defeats the purpose of these projects. Factoring in cost and usability is important for your future case modification attempts.

For the steps and procedures outlined in this chapter and in following chapters, the rotary tool made by Dremel (such as the MultiPro 275, shown in Figure 7-2) is a great cutting device for a case. Some may argue that this is the slower choice, but the focus here is on completing a window with the least amount of error. Using a rotary tool provides more control on the cutting application, and the speed helps with that. It also allows you to use different attachments, such as grinding wheels to smooth out the rough edges after cutting. Higher priced jig saws may offer orbital movement, which allows the blade to turn in different directions for tight corner cutting, but this comes at a price. Even a cheap rotary tool can accomplish this, although a bit slower.

Figure 7-2
Dremel MultiPro 275

TIPS OF THE TRADE

Which Tool Is Best for Me?

Buying a quality tool that is reliable will demand that you spend more money. It's best that you figure out your budget before jumping into this project. You do not want to purchase all your tools but end up not being able to afford the actual window!

Other companies make rotary tools, but the long history and reliability of the Dremel brand is known throughout the case modification community. The Dremel rotary comes in various models; some have adjustable speeds that range from 5000 to 35,000 rotations per minute (RPM), while others are single-speed units. While you're at the hardware store, take a look at the offerings; some may come in complete kits with a large selection of adjustable attachments. Most of the cutting projects you'll need to modify your case will require only the cut-off wheel and a grinding wheel.

Not all cutting wheels are made equal. In most rotary kits, cut-off wheels are included, but they are often brittle and thin. You may want to purchase steel mesh–reinforced wheels, which last longer and are less prone to breaking while used at high speeds. These wheels are readily available in the same aisle where you purchase your tool.

A power drill is also useful in creating a window for your case. You will need a drill as well as drill bits if you plan on using the nut-and-bolt styles of securing a window. A great drill is the DeWalt 3/8-inch, 5.4amp drill. It provides enough power to punch through most metal panels on a case. In addition to creating bolt holes, the drill can also be installed with attachments to create custom blowholes (further details on customizing the case will be provided later in the chapter).

Planning and Cutting Your Window

Adding a window to your case is somewhat like adding a new window in a wall at your house. Once the hammer hits the wall and makes the first hole, there is no turning back. This means that if your case or system is under warranty, you will definitely void it. If you are unsure about whether you want to go through with this, you might want to practice cutting a window on an older system or an empty case.

Before you make any cuts, it's a good idea to draw out the actual window design on paper and decide where it will go on the case. The size and the placement are up to you, but the usual position is on the open side of the case. This allows ample room to place a window using any of the securing methods discussed here. Common designs include circles, rectangles, and squares; custom designs such as combinations of rectangles and ovals, stars, or lightning bolts are also easily feasible. Try a simple design if this is your first time attempting this. A square or even an L-shaped window is easier to cut than an intricate star. Eventually, you will feel more comfortable with cutting metal. Do not let the square design of the case limit your imagination, because a window design can be anything you want.

Determining What You Need

The best advice for all of your projects is to measure twice and cut once. Plan ahead; it will save you time and money in the long run. Often, if you can draw out a diagram of what you want to do, it may aid you in the design of your window. Drawing to scale and measuring precisely is definitely recommended!

Designs

After you have a relative idea of what shape or shapes you want to cut, you need to measure the size of the acrylic sheet you are going to need. It's easier to buy a larger sheet in case you want to adjust the size later on. You can pick up acrylic sheets (Figure 7-3) at most major hardware stores; they are usually priced per square foot, and although prices vary, acrylic sheets are not too expensive.

Figure 7-3
Acrylic sheet

If you are working on an empty case, the first thing to do is remove the side panel of your case and place it flat on your work area. Your case may be covered by a single U-shaped case panel or individual side panels. Individual panels are easier to draw and cut into. If you have a U-shaped panel, don't worry, because you can still make a good cut. Find a shoe box or anything sturdy enough to fill in the gap between the sides within the U-shaped cover while you have it on your work area. This will give you a bit more support while you are cutting out your design.

Protect Your Investment!

Always remove the panel, even if you are working on an empty box; it's a good idea to keep the box clean, since components will be located there eventually. Cutting the case directly over components will jeopardize the functionality of your parts, since a tremendous amount of metal dust will be flying around. Try and keep the computer components clear of the work area; you never know how far metal pieces can fly when cut at 35,000 RPM.

Assuming you have an individual side panel, turn the panel around so you can see the side that faces the inside of your case. On this side, you will draw your window design with a pencil. If you are preparing a simple square or rectangle design, use your ruler to mark down the exact dimensions you need. If you are planning a more advanced shape, with ovals and other round edges, you will need a curved edge to create the curves. A spare coffee can or a compact disc should give you a large enough curve to use while penciling in the shape, or you can use a protractor. Sometimes it is best to draw a few grid lines to make it easier to position your window placement. After you have penciled in the initial design, recheck the dimensions with your ruler. Check to see whether both the left and right edges are even and uniform on the panel. A slight shift in the angle of the window will be hard to hide later on, so measure it carefully!

Cutting

With your design fully penciled in and checked and rechecked, it's time for you to determine how much of the acrylic sheet you will need for the window. Draw the shape over the adhesive paper covering the acrylic sheet. After you have the shape laid out on the sheet, you will want to add a couple of inches to expand the outline, to accommodate the attachments you'll use to mount the sheet to the case—such as Velcro or holes for nuts and bolts.

With the outline penciled in, it is time to cut the acrylic sheet to shape. If you have never used the rotary tool on acrylic, you may want to test it on a remote section of the acrylic sheet before you tackle the real thing. If you have a variable-speed tool, adjust the speed settings and see which speed is ideal for cutting through the acrylic.

Working with Your Acrylic Piece

Scoring, or precutting, the acrylic can be helpful as an aid. If you have a straight edge, you can break off the piece at the score by using this method. Some people prefer to score the sheet with a hobby knife before cutting with the rotary tool. This is up to you—if you feel comfortable cutting it right off the bat, go for it.

As an added protection against scratching and mistakes, add a couple layers of masking tape on the inside of the penciled outline. In case of a sudden jerky movement from the tool, the masking tape can prevent a scratch from marking the acrylic. You may want to work outdoors while cutting this sheet, since cutting the plastic will emit an odor.

When you are ready, cut along the outline slowly and evenly. If the acrylic is melting, slow down or stop cutting to allow the area to cool down. Take your time, and soon you will have cut an acrylic sheet to your shape.

After the acrylic sheet is cut to size, place it against the panel to see if all edges are covering your penciled outline. If everything matches up correctly, you can proceed to cutting the metal case.

Always be cautious and utilize all safety equipment before you make any cuts. Change the cut-off wheel if it is an unusable size at this time. Mask off the area outside of the outline you drew on the side panel with two layers of masking tape. This will prevent any scratches that may occur if you stray from the cutting area. Since you will not be using the portion inside the panel and nobody will see it, you don't need to cover that with masking tape. Keep in mind that the metal is a lot harder than the acrylic, so adjust your rotary tool if necessary to compensate.

You can cut through the metal in two ways: you can slowly cut through the outline or lightly cut in layers. The latter method will take you longer, but it will give you a cleaner cut. Figure 7-4 shows the side panel cut out.

Figure 7-4
Cutting the metal
side panel

Once the entire section of the window has been cut out, you will want to smooth out the rough edges. Leave your gloves on and remove the cut-off wheel from your rotary tool. Be careful not to run your fingers across any rough edges; it may cut you. Attach a grinding or sanding attachment and run it back and forth over the edges to remove any sharp edges. If you are using a jig saw or you don't have a grinding attachment, you can use some sandpaper to smooth out the edges.

Securing the Acrylic

Now you can place the acrylic piece on your panel to check for size differences. If you're using Velcro, nuts and bolts, or rivets, the acrylic piece should be larger than the shape cut into the metal panel by a couple of inches. By this point, you should have a good idea of how you're going to secure your acrylic to the metal panel. The extra inches you left on the acrylic sheet will allow you to use any of the following methods:

❑ Velcro/chrome car trim

❑ Nuts and bolts

❑ Rivets

❑ Rubber molding

If you want a transparent design, Velcro (Figure 7-5) is the easiest method to use. You can purchase Velcro sheets with adhesive backings at hardware and craft shops. The advantage of Velcro is that you can adjust it whenever you wish. If you have cut a square window design, attach two to four strips on each edge between the window and the panel. The window should stay in place with little or no movement. If you make a mistake, just remove the window and reattach it on the Velcro strip.

Figure 7-5
Velcro

Using chrome car trim (Figure 7-6) requires the incorporation of Velcro. Car trim is available at any auto shop, usually for less than $5 a foot. The trim usually goes around the edges of a car door or other edges to give it a shiny look. You can use chrome trim to line the outer edge of your metal side panel you just cut. This gives it a cleaner finish, as opposed to the bare edge cut. The trim itself comes in a U-shape that slips around the edge of your cut, with a small adhesive lining on the inside to keep it in place; it is extremely easy to secure. Once you have the chrome lining attached, just secure the window against the metals side panel with the Velcro technique.

Figure 7-6
Chrome car trim

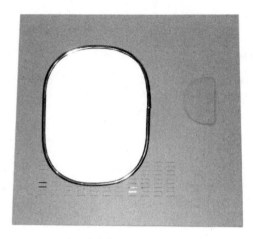

Using nuts and bolts (Figure 7-7) to secure the window will require that you drill holes at different points on the panel and the acrylic sheet. You can purchase nuts and bolts at any hardware store, and they should not cost more than $3 for a handful. Depending on your window size, choose a nut size that is not too large. You do not want to make the nuts and bolts the main attraction on your case—that's what your window is for. A ¼-inch size or less is adequate in most window designs.

Figure 7-7
Nuts and bolts

Before you drill holes into your acrylic sheet and side panel, you need to figure out where you are going to put them. With four-sided windows, one in each corner will be needed. If it is a large rectangle, more holes in between the corners will be needed. First, you should measure where the holes will be placed on the metal panel.

After you have the right-sized nut and bolt combination and you've penciled-in the hole marks, use a power drill with the corresponding sized drill bit to drill holes through the metal cover. Remember to drill on the side of the panel that is facing the inside of the case.

Do Not Take Shortcuts

Do not drill the acrylic sandwiched on the metal side panel. You can ruin the acrylic and scratch the metal if you take this shortcut. Separate the two pieces and measure out each corresponding hole. Drill them independently making sure after each attempt to check your drilling positions.

After you have drilled the holes in the panel, flip the panel over and place it over the acrylic sheet. Line up the acrylic sheet against the panel opening. With a marker, add dots on the acrylic through the holes you drilled on the metal side panel. Lift the panel off the acrylic, and all the corresponding holes should be marked and ready to drill. Slowly drill a single bolt hole through the acrylic. Do not run it through too fast, or you may risk cracking the surrounding area. As always, "measure twice and cut once" is the rule during this phase of the project.

After drilling one hole, place the metal side panel on top of the acrylic again to determine whether all the holes are matched up correctly. Adjust accordingly if the sizing is slightly off. Remove the panel and continue drilling the other holes in the acrylic sheet. If you have never used a power drill, you may also use the masking tape method to protect the acrylic sheet. When all the holes are drilled, line up the metal side panel and acrylic and screw the bolts down to finish the window modification.

Rivets can also be used to secure the window. Rivets are most likely used to secure the stationary pieces of metal on your case, so you might check them out to see if you want to use them to attach your window. If you want to use rivets to secure your case window, you can purchase some rivets and a rivet tool for about $35 at your local hardware store.

You will need to drill holes first on the metal side panel and acrylic window as with nuts and bolts. Use the size of the rivets you are using as a guide for the size of the holes. Once the holes have been drilled, run the rivets through them and fasten the window to the panel.

Rubber molding (Figure 7-8) is probably the most widely used method of fastening a window to a case. It is similar to the chrome car trim, in that it lines the outer edge of the window design you cut from the metal side panel. Rubber molding was originally used as a seal for windows in homes, but it has since been modified to cater to window modifications. The originals were U-shaped, just like car trim. You may be able to pick up some molding at the local hardware store, but often you will be met with confused stares from the employees. It is easier and cheaper to pick some up from online case-modification retailers. About 3 feet of the molding will run approximately $6 to $7.

Figure 7-8
Rubber molding

Using rubber molding is a little different than using the previous methods. Instead of adding extra space in your acrylic for attaching, you will need to subtract a little. The acrylic shape will need to be about ¼-inch smaller than the window opening in the panel to make room for the molding.

The molding comes in black, usually with a separate locking strip. The strip is round in shape with three cuts on the side. The side facing inward has a cut channel for the locking strip, while another two cuts channel to fit the edges of the metal side panel and the acrylic window. Slide the acrylic window inside the molding and fit the molding over the edges of the case. Once you have it fitted, take the locking strip and slide it into the open locking strip channel and you will have finished your rubber molding–lined window modification.

Getting some Extra Leverage

If you have trouble fitting the edges of the metal side panel and your acrylic sheet into the molding, you can use a screwdriver as an aid to guide the edges of either along the channel. Be careful not to scratch the acrylic or metal surface!

After you have installed your window, you can add lights and other accessories to further enhance the case. This will be covered in the next chapter.

Should I Use Rubber Molding?

One of the beauties of using any type of molding is its capability to hide any marks or scratches on the edges of your window. This gives you a little extra breathing room in case you make a slight cutting mistake. The rubber molding is also easy to maneuver around edges that can help in custom oval- or circular-shaped windows.

Window Variations

Along with installing a window on a side panel, you can add other variations to the theme. As long as you have enough room, another window can be installed on the case—for example, on the top panel. It is both interesting and eerie to look down and see through your case. The cutting and securing methods described so far can all be used to install a top panel window. The top panel will often not be removable like the side panel, so you will need to remove any components inside the case before attempting to cut the metal.

With the top window installed in a tower, you will most likely be viewing the optical drives (CD-ROM, DVD, and so on). Another modification that is becoming popular is adding smaller-sized windows within an optical drive, and sometimes within hard drives! The same methodology is used to put together a window in your drive. You may be able to use the extra pieces of acrylic from your metal side panel window. Sometimes this may not work, however, because of the thickness of the acrylic space at the top cover of an optical drive is extremely limited.

What About Warranties?

Be careful with opening any of your storage devices, because doing so will definitely void any warranties that you may have with the manufacturer! If you are unsure whether or not your warranty has expired, consult the documentation that came with your drive or system. Sometimes, the drive itself has a date stamp that tells you when the warranty expires.

Remove the screws on the optical drive and remove the top cover. As you did for the side panel, create a simple design and follow the same cutting procedures. Measure with a ruler to ensure that the window will cover the compact disc area. To secure it, you may need to use some sort of glue. Putting Velcro there may cause the case not to close because of the extra height; this goes for nuts and bolts as well. Replace the cover and attach everything back together.

You can do the exact same modification to a hard drive. If you are nervous about opening up these drives, you may want to practice first on an older spare drive.

Windows can also be installed in many other places. You can even modify a mouse to have a small window! As long as a component has enough space, you can add a window.

Window Accessories

After you have created and installed a window, you can add lights to the mix or even add a custom etching into the acrylic. If etching is not your cup of tea, you can always try a sticker application. Or you can add in an intake or exhaust hole to help cool the interior components. You have many options from which to choose, including some easy and aesthetically pleasing varieties discussed here.

30 TO 45 MINUTES

Using a rotary tool, or 10 minutes using a hole saw attachment on a power drill

Creating a Blowhole

Where your side panel acrylic window is located is directly over where the processor and motherboard are located. This area is usually high in temperature due to the processor and video card working hard—this is especially true when they are both stressed in gaming situations. To counteract this problem, you can create a ventilation hole over the processor area. The ventilation hole, or blowhole, will utilize a powered fan either to bring in cool air or exhaust hot air. This example brings in cool air from the outside and is called an *intake* hole.

Here is what you will need to obtain before you start:

- ❑ 80, 92, or 120mm case fan
- ❑ Fan grill
- ❑ Fan screws

If the acrylic window is already attached to your panel, you should remove it now. If you used Velcro, this should be easy, and you can reattach it later.

Before you start cutting again, you need to figure out what size fan you'll use. In this example, a 120mm fan will be installed into an acrylic window. If you follow the lead here, a 120mm fan has a clearance circle equivalent to the diameter of a compact disc. Obtain a spare compact disc and use it to trace an outline where you want the blowhole to be located. An erasable marker is fine to use for marking the outline. The placement of the hole is up to you, since each case is different, but the most useful area is near the processor and video card.

After you've drawn the outline, you need to mask off the area as before, using masking tape. This will prevent any marks that may occur if you slip while cutting the blowhole. You can use your rotary tool to cut out the blowhole.

If you are planning on adding more blowholes in different places on your case, a hole saw (Figure 7-9) might be a good choice—they're available at your local hardware store. A hole saw can cut an exact size to fit most case fan sizes.

Figure 7-9
Hole saws

If you decide to use a smaller-sized fan, such as a 80 or 92mm, you can use a fan grill as a guide to draw the blowhole or purchase the corresponding hole saw attachment. Fan grills are metal grills intended to stop foreign objects from moving into the fan. Grills are sized in relation to the size of the fan for which they are made.

After removing the cut-out blowhole, line up your fan grill to make sure the hole is the correct size. Use your rotary tool to smooth out the edges if needed. If you are satisfied with the design and cut, take a marker and mark four dots where the fan grill will be attached using screws. Find the correct sized drill by sliding a few bits through the fan grill's screw holes until the size matches. Mask off the drill area, if needed, and punch through four holes, one by one. Be sure to check between drilling each hole to make sure it is oriented correctly. After you've punched all the screw holes, place the grill on the outside of the acrylic window and the fan on the inside. Screw the four fan screws through and tighten until secured. You have just installed your first intake blowhole, and it should look something like Figure 7-10.

Figure 7-10
Blowhole with grill

Window Etching and Sticker Applications

Etching the acrylic will require the use of your rotary tool with a sanding attachment to etch a design into the surface of the acrylic. A sticker application is easier and can be removed later. Both offer interesting finishing touches to a window modification.

Etching acrylic is similar to normal wood work. Small scratches are made onto the surface of the window to create a somewhat blurred design. Any design is possible, ranging from letters to pictures. As with any project, you will need to plan where and what you are etching before you pick up a tool. You will also need some sort of back lighting or else you will not be able to see your etching clearly. You can mark the acrylic panel with an erasable marker; since the area where you mark will be etched, the markings will not show through later on. Lightly scratch the surface where you marked until you see a slight blurred mark. It's best to scratch in layers, starting shallow at first—if you do it all in one attempt, some sections of the etching may be deeper than others. Clean off the area frequently, and you should be able to see your creation as you work. The etched surface of your acrylic should look something like Figure 7-11.

Figure 7-11
Etching surface

If marking the acrylic is something you do not want to do, you can print out or buy transparent adhesive stickers and apply them to the window instead. Numerous online retailers offer premade sticker applications and will do custom work. A sample sticker application is shown in Figure 7-12.

Figure 7-12
Application sample

Where Do You Go from Here?

The steps provided here are not the absolute rules for window construction. Numerous alternatives can be used for the classic acrylic window; just let your imagination shape the way your box looks and feels. You can substitute a colored acrylic window for the clear version, for example. Blowholes can be added in different positions as well as in numbers. In the next chapter, different options of lighting will be explored, to further enhance your case window.

If these raw materials are not available in your area, you can purchase most of them online. Since case modification has reached a lot of mainstream retailers, you can often purchase the tools at local computer shops. These online and local shops should carry case fans as well as the fan accessories needed.

TESTING 1-2-3

❏ After the window has been cut and installed, you should wipe down your side panel to clear away any debris.

❏ Make sure all metal fragments are removed on both sides of the panel. Install your panel on your case to make sure that it fits in place.

❏ If you used the nut-and-bolt method and the bolts are too long, you can shorten them with your rotary tool. Take the necessary precautions before doing this, just as you did when cutting the window.

❏ If you made a mistake on your acrylic window and it is not usable, don't throw it away. You can use the remaining usable sections to try a smaller window mod.

Chapter 8

Case Lighting

Tools of the Trade

Wire cutter/stripper
Scissors
Small screwdrivers
Hobby knife
Pliers
Molex connectors
Switches
Wires
Neon tube(s)
Cold cathode fluorescent lamp(s)
Electro luminescent light(s)
Electrical tape
Heatshrink
Heat gun/hair dryer

You can make your own distinct case modifications in any number of ways. Chapter 7 detailed window construction and embellishment, and this chapter continues the customization process.

With the addition of light, the hardware inside your case can be "showcased" to create a dramatic effect. You can spend hundreds, if not thousands, of dollars putting together a performance computer system. After you've spent the time and money required to build a powerful system, including a light source can add a little more spice to the mix to solidify your feeling of achievement when another user compliments you on your system.

Case modders have an assortment of light options at their disposal. Before we venture into each option, you will need to be familiar with the basic tools you'll use to get your project off the ground: scissors, a hobby knife, electrical wires, power connectors, electrical tape or heatshrink, and switches. If you would like to implement more advanced case modifications, you may need the following equipment: a rotary tool or drill, wire stripper, heat gun, and soldering iron. These items can be purchased at your local hardware store and electronics shop.

TIPS OF THE TRADE

Can't Find What You Need?

If your local shops do not have the accessories or parts needed to install a lighting system, numerous online electronics vendors can supply parts to help mod your system. Some reliable vendors are allelectronics.com and jameco.com. Both have a huge catalog that should have everything you need for our projects.

This chapter discusses several types of lights that are easy to obtain at many retail stores. Your choices are almost infinite in regard to size and color preferences. Before we begin, note that the steps described here are by no means highly technical. The chapter is not meant to confuse you with technical terms; better that you spend time getting your own system up and running and learning specific techniques rather than struggle through technical electronics issues.

Introduction to Case Lighting

Let's start by getting familiar with how these lights are powered. Within a case, the power supply provides voltage at 12V. As long as you purchase your items and abide by that voltage, you will be able to turn them on. The simplest way to get power to most units within your case is through the use of a Molex connector. The Molex, or 4-pin, connector (shown in Figure 8-1) is a standard for most computer powering units such as hard drives and CD-ROM drives. The connector provides a 12V DC line, two ground lines, and a 5V line. We will concentrate on using the 12V DC throughout this chapter.

Figure 8-1
The Molex connector

The beauty of using these connectors is that they can be chained together to provide power for numerous components. As long as your power supply can provide enough power, these connectors will support the task at hand.

Have Enough Power?

All components that require power will draw it from your power supply. Choose a higher wattage power supply if you plan on adding a larger number of lights in your case. Not having enough power can cause your components to function improperly. Refer to Chapter 1 for more information about power supply levels.

Neon Tubes

The first and most common lighting choice among case modders is the neon tube. With sizes varying from 10 to 20 inches, you can provide enough light inside your case to make interesting effects and start you off on your case lighting journey. When it was still a new technology, neon lighting was used mainly in storefronts as an advertising medium. Neon lights are gas-filled tubes that change color as a result of metal electrodes on each end being charged with a high voltage. Different gases within the tube at low pressure will give off different color when this charging takes place, offering an easy way to add color to any sign or display. Neon lights later evolved into singular tubes, smaller in size for smaller applications. The new portable design of these 10-to-15-inch tubes became popular with the automotive scene, offering colored light in small spaces inside cars. Their main appeal is that they work well in both lit and dark areas, which is exactly what we are looking for.

Many retailers currently provide preassembled neon kits specifically made for the computer case. This chapter takes an alternative route in an effort to save you some money. The most convenient place to obtain a neon tube will probably be at your local auto parts and accessories store. Auto shops stock a wide variety of sizes and shapes, as well as units that are sound activated and that pulse depending on how loud you have music playing. You can also try local hobby shops, which may carry the same items. The main problems with these units are that they come prewired for automobile use through a cigarette lighter. Even so, you can get them working in your case with a little modification. Measure your case before you purchase a neon tube to see which size will fit best.

After you have acquired a tube, you will need to get the necessary accessories to get power to the unit. The simplest way to make these tubes light up within your case is to use a Molex (4-pin) power connector and wire it directly into your neon tube. You can pick up these connectors at most electronics shops. They are extremely affordable, and you may wish to pick them up in packs. If you obtained your tube from an auto shop, cut off the portion that's supposed to connect to the cigarette lighter adapter. You'll be connecting the wires to the Moles connector instead.

Each tube will have two wires—the 12V DC line and the ground wire. If you refer back to Figure 8-1, there are four wires. The yellow wire indicates 12V, red indicates 5V, and the two black wires are ground. You will wire up the 12V DC/ground wires from the neon tube to the yellow and black wires from the molex connector. Leave yourself enough wire to work with since you will be connecting the wires together.

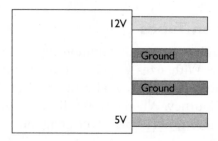

After you have split the wires from the neon tube, determine which wire is the 12V DC and which is the ground. With most tube wires, a white stripe runs down the 12V DC wire, while the ground wire has no markings. To connect the 12V and ground wires of the neon tube to the Molex connector, you first need to strip each end on each wire. A wire stripper comes in handy, or you can use a hobby knife or scissors to remove the plastic covers on the wires. Most of the time, the bare wire underneath will be copper or silver stranded. You might see a solid, single-core wire, but that's a rarity; plus, these types of wire do not last when bent repeatedly.

The next step would be to twist together the bare wire leads of the neon tube and wrap them in electrical tape, or—the professional way—soldering both ends and heatshrinking them together.

Maximum Heat

Make sure you have enough space to work with, and be careful of the heat from your soldering iron. Ideally, the iron should not exceed more than 15W, because a higher wattage iron will run the risk of injury or damage to components.

Before sealing the two bare leads with solder, slip a small section of heatshrink onto the wire and move it away from the bare wire area. Heatshrink is a great alternative to electrical tape, since it wraps securely without the adhesive residue that electrical tape can leave behind over time. Just make sure to purchase a heatshrink tube size that's the same size as the wire gauge you're using in your project.

With the bare leads exposed, drop a few beads of solder onto the area and be sure it makes a solid connection. Once that has cooled down and solidified, slide the heatshrink over the connected area. Then hold the heat gun about 2 inches away from the heatshrink tube for a few seconds. The heatshrink should contract and hold onto the wires tightly. With the wires connected, you now have a neon tube wired to the Molex connector and ready to be installed.

Securing the Connection

If a heat gun is not accessible, a hair dryer can be used as a substitute. Make sure not to heat the heatshrink for prolonged periods of time, because they can melt!

Before installing the neon light into your case, turn off the computer and unplug the main power cord to your power supply. Position the neon tube and plug the Molex connector into an available spot from your power supply. The most common area is at the bottom of the case, which has the most room. Plug in the power cord and turn on your computer. If all connections are secure, you should see a nicely lit interior through your case window, as shown in Figure 8-2.

Figure 8-2
Neon tube installed

Motherboards and other components are offered in a variety of colors nowadays. The bland green printed circuit boards (PCBs) are gone, with such colors as red, black, and white now appearing on the market. This opens up the field for different color combinations that best compliment your own system. For example, installing a red neon tube with a computer system comprising red components will stand out far better than one that is built around the standard green. Keep color in mind when designing your own case lighting environment.

Electro Luminescent Light

You'll find neon available in different shapes. Changes in case design have paved the way for changes in neon applications. Neons help spawn variations such as electro luminescent (EL) cables, which operate just like neon tubes except at about a fraction of the size. These cables are about 3/32 of an inch in width and provide about the same amount of light as a neon tube. The cables also vary in brightness, depending on how much power is provided to them through the use of an AC inverter, which converts the power needed through the use of your power supply within the case.

One major advantage of EL cable is the flexibility it has over conventional neon tubes. Regular neon tubes cannot bend at all, but EL cable can bend around corners and edges. It gives you complete control over where you want to place light in a case and with how much brightness. If the thin, rounded cable is not what you need, you can find flat EL tape lights (Figure 8-3) that work exactly the same. They often come with an adhesive backing that lets you stick the tape lights onto walls and around edges inside the case. Both of these types of lights are powered by an inverter, which is commonly connected to a Molex plug as in our previous examples.

Figure 8-3
EL tape light

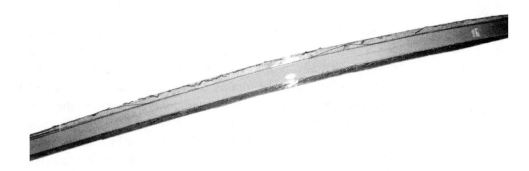

Cold Cathode Fluorescent Lamp

A newer and thinner variation on the neon theme was introduced not too long ago to the case modding market. Cold cathode fluorescent lamps (CCFLs), shown in Figure 8-4, have been around since the early 1900s. The CCFLs are called *cold cathodes* mainly because they lack a filament like most fluorescent lamps. This, in turn, makes the lamp produce less heat—but do not be fooled, because these lamps are still warm to the touch. Mercury gases, as well as other gases, are mixed together inside the glass tube. A phosphorus coating is applied around the tube that reacts to the ultraviolet (UV) energy given off when the electrode ends of the tube are charged. This reaction creates a bright white light.

You may not realize it, but a lot of today's electronics function with the aid of CCFLs. Many liquid crystal displays (LCDs) use CCFLs to provide back lighting so you can view computer and video screens in the dark. Scanners use them for a source of light when scanning images to your computer. Without confusing you with all the technical information on how CCFLs work, we will try and explain the process.

Since bright white light is not exactly the ideal color to make heads turn, different combinations of phosphorus can be applied to create different colors. Only three main colors—red, blue, and green—are available with CCFLs (other colors can be created by mixing these three). Because the CCFL has no filament, it can take a bit more abuse than a normal fluorescent lamp. Even so, a protective cover should be used. Acrylic tubes generally are the ideal solution to use as protective barriers because they are clear. The CCFL glass tubes measure only about a ¼ inch, which makes them very fragile when not protected. Like neon tubes, CCFL tubing is not bendable, but recent advancements have made different shapes possible in production.

With the speed at which the case modification market operates, CCFLs were quick hits. Most case modders do not worry only about looks, but also about system performance—and the number one enemy is heat. Neon tubes require more power, which in turn creates a bit more heat than CCFLs. That reasoning alone makes the cold cathode solution a better choice among many case modders. Some may also argue that the cold cathodes are brighter than neons, and if compared in size, the cold cathodes are smaller and easier to use. At the present time, many retailers offer CCFL kits prewired with switches and Molex connectors, much like their neon counterparts. Installing one is pretty much a plug-and-play situation, but we want to mimic our neon example design and install it into our own case.

Cold cathodes require the use of an inverter to convert 12V DC, which is what your power supply outputs, to 1000V AC. Note the changes between *AC* and *DC* power through the inverter.

When purchasing your CCFL, you can opt for the prewired units or purchase a bare kit. Bare kits are widely available at electronics shops online and through local hobby stores. We focus on the installation of bare kits simply because they are remarkably cheaper.

After you have secured a unit, check to see that two wires emerge from your cold cathode tube and that an extra set of 12V DC wires are included as well. Notice the difference in the size of wires that come from the tube; they are a lot thicker and better insulated to support the higher voltage. Make sure that you have an inverter.

You should see two connection points on either side of the small inverter. Connect the cold cathode tube on one end and connect your bare 12V DC leads to the other. Secure a Molex connector and wire it up to the bare leads of the 12V DC wires and insulate them well with electrical tape or heatshrink. You can adjust the wiring and include a switch to turn this light on and off.

To Dim or Not to Dim

Keep in mind that it's not a good idea to adjust or dim your cold cathode. The CCFL tubes can go as low as 7V, which is not recommended. Dimming is often accomplished by limiting the amount of voltage going towards powering the light. Neon tubes and CCFL tubes all have a point where the light will go out. Using them at these lower voltages over time can cause damage and lead to power-on failure.

After the Molex and wires have been fully insulated, you may also want to consider insulating the inverter. Most of these bare units are not insulated, so covering the inverter may prevent shortages or shock when you're handling your wired unit. Some retailers offer these tubes with acrylic or plastic covers that help protect the glass. It's a good idea to pick up a cover if yours didn't come with one.

As with neon, the positioning of the light is up to you. Often, the bottom of the case will provide the maximum space for most light applications. Designing lighting can be tricky, so it is best that you plan out exactly what you want to accomplish. For example, if you are modifying a full tower, a single CCFL tube will not provide enough light. You may want to invest in two or three to get the job done. When you've selected the best position, you can get double-sided foam tape, Velcro, or zip ties to hang the tubes on the top or sides of your case. These methods also work with neon tubes; adjust the size needed with the adhesives accordingly.

30 TO 60 MINUTES

Take Control of Your Light

The design with a single Molex connector powering the tube works well if you don't mind having the light on all the time that your computer is running. But if your machine needs to be on and the neon light needs to be off, you might want to include an on-and-off switch to control the unit.

To accomplish this, you can install a switch on the power line between the power supply and neon tube. An SPST (single pole, single throw) switch (Figure 8-5) can be purchased at any electronics store, and they come in a variety of colors. This switch controls the current powering the tube. It offers on and off positions and is ideal for this application.

Figure 8-5
SPST switch

To make the switch function, you will need to wire the leads (as explained earlier) onto the switch itself. Think of it as a connection point in the flow of power. When the switch is in the off position, the power is cut off and the tube's light goes out. When the switch is in the on position, power is continued over to the tube, causing it to turn on. It's a simple design that gets the job done.

You can use other ways to control the amount of light from your neon. Rheostats, which act like dialed switches, allow precise control over how much power is provided to the tube at any time. This allows for dimming of the tube to a certain degree, much like a volume control knob on a stereo receiver. As mentioned earlier, this is not recommended and can cause damage to your lighting.

Wiring a switch follows the same route as wiring it up directly with a Molex (see the following illustration). Take the bare leads from the 12V DC on the Molex and connect it to the *on* position prong, and wire the 12V DC line from the neon tube to the *off* position prong. The ground will stay connected from the Molex to the tube. After the wires have been connected, you need to position the switch somewhere accessible. No sense in creating a controlling mechanism if you can't get to it.

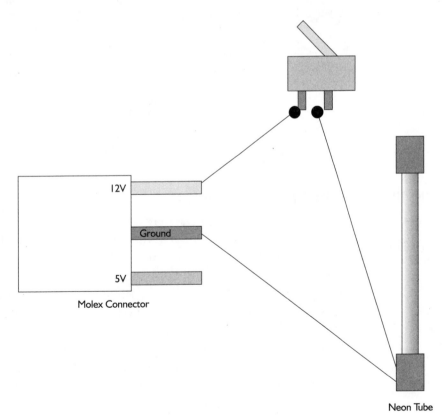

12V

Ground

5V

Molex Connector

Neon Tube

You can install the switch in a couple of places: one of the more common areas is the 5¼-inch bay expansion plates on the front bezel, or front panel, of the case. The switch will have a nut that comes loose at the base of the toggle. Before drilling anything, measure and draw the hole. This will help you make multiple switch installations more uniform in a row. Find the matching-sized drill bit that will allow the SPST (on/off) switch to fit through a hole and drill the hole. The nut that you removed will go over the switch and tighten itself against the bay cover.

Switches come in different styles and sizes, and they range from standard metal toggle designs to flat black plastic lever styles. Just keep in mind that any switch that can continue or break a connection in a power line will work in this design. Figure 8-6 shows several switches lined up in the bay.

Figure 8-6
Switches in the bay

30 TO 90 MINUTES   Light-Emitting Diodes

About 30 to 90 minutes depending on which LED project you choose to do

Light-emitting diodes (LEDs) may not be a top choice among case modders, but the LED has been around for years and is relatively cheap. Invented in the 1960s, LEDs have become a staple in our everyday lives. They are used to signify different stages in electronics and appliances with yellow, red, or green lights. LEDs are a lot like tiny light bulbs without filaments. Due to this construction, the tiny bulbs are less prone to burning out and produce very little heat. The light emitted from LEDs is caused by fast moving electrons within the bulb.

LEDs come in various sizes to fit various applications. The more common size is the 3mm or 5mm bulbs, which are used throughout a case. The intensity of the light is measured in MCD (mill candelas). The higher the MCD rating, the brighter your LED will be.

Before you learn what you can do with these tiny bulbs, you need to know a little bit about their basic design. All LEDs have two leads that protrude from the bottom of the dome. One lead is always longer, which tells you that it's the anode (+), while the shorter lead is the cathode (–). Although it won't damage anything, wiring LED leads in the wrong orientation will cause the bulb not to light up.

Prepare your workspace, and have a small tray on hand to hold your screws and LEDs while you work. Locate Philips and flathead screwdrivers and warm up your soldering iron. We will replace some of the stock LEDs in the case as well as those in the accessories in your machine—such as speakers, keyboards, floppy drives, and optical drives.

Front bezels will be the easiest place to start this journey. On a case, you'll see at least two or three LEDs that display power and hard drive use. Some of these flash, while others stay lit as long as power is on. These stock bulbs shine at a minimal intensity and give off a weak yellow or green color. To adjust this, find some higher-rated LEDs in any other color you wish. For this purpose, we chose blue because it shines incredibly well in the dark.

First, power down the whole system; you definitely do not want to work with anything electrical while your system is turned on. Then remove the front bezel (face) from your case. You may notice that wires are attached to internal components—if so, trace them back inside the case and remove them so the front bezel can be disconnected. On the back side of the bezel, find where the stock LEDs are and push them forward or backward to loosen them. Once removed, measure your new LEDs against the old ones to determine the right length to trim your bare leads. After figuring out the ideal length, trim the leads and curl the tips into a tiny loop. Note that most LEDs (shown in Figure 8-7) have extra long leads, so trimming them will aid you in installing them into the stock position later.

Figure 8-7
Bare LED

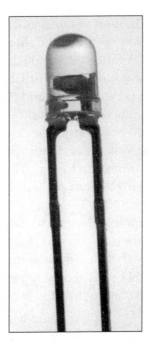

Remember the correct orientation of the cathode and anode; it will save a lot of time if you do this right on the first try. Clip and strip the ends of the wire that were on the old LEDs and solder them onto the new loops you just made. To tidy and insulate the newly soldered area, you can apply a layer of electrical tape or heatshrink, both of which will work nicely in this situation. Push back the new LEDs into the front panel and reinstall the wires if you need to. Power on your computer; if all connections are complete, the front bezel will definitely look different to you.

Let's move on to the next replacement: the speaker. Most high-powered speakers have a LED that shines when the unit is turned on. Instead of the pale yellow or green, we'll switch the stock LEDs to blue ones. Like all of our projects, unplug the power first, and place all the items on a clean work area. Prepare yourself with the screwdriver and soldering iron. Your speaker's design will determine whether these instructions work; we're providing a general outline here, but you may need to be more ingenious with your speaker assembly routine. You will need to locate the speaker where the LED is installed and find the screws that hold it together. Unscrew the bottom or top until you have access to the circuit board and speaker inside the housing.

At this point, you may notice that the LED is free standing on top of the circuit board. Also note that the LED itself may be the smaller 3mm-sized bulb due to the space limitations within the speaker housing. To get a new blue LED into the speaker, you will either have to purchase some smaller 3mm-sized LEDs or take the 5mm unit and shave it down to size. This can be accomplished by sanding the bulb with sandpaper until you achieve the correct size.

Once you have sized the LED correctly, take your soldering iron and lightly touch the bottom of the circuit board, where the leads from the stock bulb are attached. Do not leave the soldering iron on the board for too long, or it will damage it. While you are touching the soldered points, loosen the old bulb by rocking it back and forth until it pops out. As in our previous example, measure the length as best you can and clip the bare leads. Position the new LED into the two holes where the old bulb was and drop some solder into it with the iron. This should bond rather quickly and hold the new LEDs in place. As for orientation, just look at the circuit board where the leads go in and you will see a plus (+) sign for the anode lead. Work backward and screw on all the panels and parts. Fire up the system and check to see if the new LED is working properly (see Figure 8-8).

At this point, you may wonder why some LED packages tell you that they operate at certain voltages, yet the two processes outlined here are simply plug and play. This is because most of these components have built-in resistors that prevent the LED from getting too much power. As long as the component you own has an LED, more than likely any other LED will work just fine in its place.

Figure 8-8
Free standing LED
on keyboard (PCB)

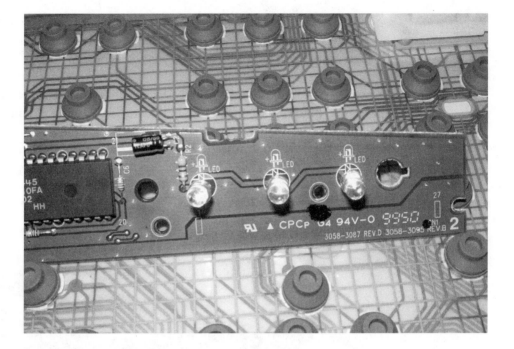

The last item on the project list is changing out the LED within the floppy drive or optical drive. The floppy drive will usually flash while it is accessing data from your disk. Optical drives such as the CD-ROM, DVD, and CD-RW may stay on or flash like the floppy during data access. Although floppy and optical drive architecture are quite different, the underlying process of replacing these status LEDs on the front are nearly identical. Please follow all precautions and unplug any power sources if you are going to work on any of your hardware components.

Before you start, you will need to remove either drive from the case if you have not done so already. Unplug any wires and place the drive on an open workspace. Both types of drive will have a plastic front faceplate covering the internals of the drive; you will need to look on the left and right sides and locate a set of tabs that lock the front faceplate into place. Take a small pen or screwdriver and give it a gentle push; this will loosen it enough so you can pull off the front cover. Proceed to flip over the drive to its underside, and locate the screws holding the metal pieces together. Unscrew them and remove the metal cover to reveal the circuit board inside.

Usually, the LED is positioned near the front, so give yourself enough room to maneuver. You may wish to remove the circuit board from the metal covering if you cannot access the LED. Once you locate the stock LED, follow the steps outlined earlier on how to remove it. Measure the new LED you will be putting in against the old one to determine the length needed for the leads. Take the soldering iron and solder the leads onto the circuit board. Check to ensure that the anode and cathode leads are oriented correctly. Check the circuit board for an indication of this; otherwise, you will need to check the stock LED to determine which end goes where.

Some of these drives may have square- (Figure 8-9) or rectangle-shaped LEDs. They are custom fit into the front bezel, but that should not cause a problem. You simply need to enlarge the plastic where the LED will fit. A pair of pliers or even a utility knife will work. Before closing the casing and screwing everything back together, check the solder points for a strong bond. If everything checks out, put everything back together. Plug all your wires back in and enjoy your final product.

Figure 8-9
Floppy, square LED

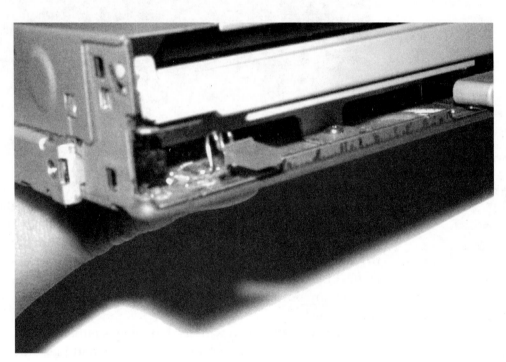

LEDs can also be used as accent lighting for small areas within your case. This can add a different feel because of the small radius of bright colored light the LED can emit.

You can use the steps outlined here to replace just about any LED you have in your system.

Is this Safe on My Components?

Note that modifying your LEDs will probably void any warranties with your equipment manufacturers. And as with all the procedures in this book, the procedures mentioned here should always be attempted in a safe environment with proper preparation.

❏ The most difficult portion of each project is putting back together the device that you just opened. Keeping all components together will make it easy to replace each piece in reverse order.

❏ Keep all the screws and small parts from your floppy or optical drive in a cup or tray. This will help you find the pieces quickly later on.

❏ Check the light after completion; if it flickers or does not turn on, check your power connections.

❏ Make sure that all bare leads are insulated with tape or heatshrink. This will prevent any unnecessary power shorts.

Chapter 9
Painting Techniques

Tools of the Trade

Two to three cans of spray paint, any color

One can of primer

One can of clear coat

A couple sheets of 320 to 600 grit wet/dry sandpaper

Sanding block

Drill with various-sized drill bits

Goggles

Face mask

Clean towels

Rubbing compound (optional)

Soap and water or alcohol (optional)

Vinyl dye (optional)

Small screwdriver (optional)

Now that you've installed case windows and numerous lighting options, it's time to paint your case. Most stock cases come in the boring beige or off-white color that everyone takes for granted. Beige cases have been the standard up until recently; finally, manufacturers have taken notice of the modification scene and are designing cases with more interesting colors. Instead of purchasing a colored case designed by some company, you can paint your own case in an interesting way to make it look great and unique (see Figure 9-1).

Not only can you apply full paint jobs, but you can also do custom designs that stock cases do not offer.

Figure 9-1
A painted case

In this chapter, you'll learn about some ways to paint your case a different color. With so many different types of paints available, and numerous ways to apply them, we can't cover it all in one chapter. Our aim is to break the painting process down into easy-to-follow steps.

ONE HOUR ## Choosing a Work Space

As with creating case windows, the most important step in painting is preparation. Before you begin, you should figure out where you want to paint. Your work space is just as important as the color of the paint you choose. You will need a well-ventilated area with very little disturbance in the air. Painting indoors is probably the best option, as long as you find a place that can provide good ventilation for the paint fumes. A garage is ideal if you are going the indoor route. Patios and backyards are also usable for outdoor solutions, but you run the risk of wind blowing your paint around or blowing dust and other airborne materials into the paint.

Find an area that will provide a constant temperature of over 60 degrees Fahrenheit. Any colder, and the sprayed layers will have a hard time drying. Make sure that you lay out paper on the floor if you are painting on a surface you do not want to stain. The last thing you want to do after completing a perfect painting project is scrubbing the floor clean of paint.

Pick the Right Spot

You should also make sure that a good light source is available in your work space. If you paint in a dimly lit area, you probably won't apply paint evenly over the case, creating heavy spots in some areas of your case while not having enough paint to cover others spots.

Preparing the Case

Once you have found an ideal work space, you'll need to prepare your case. If the case is currently intact, remove all of its components first. Remove each piece of the case that you want to paint. If the top piece of your case is riveted shut, use a drill to punch a hole through the rivets. You can fasten the top later on with screws instead.

Wipe down your case inside and out with a damp cloth to remove any dust. You can also use soap and water to clean the surface, or use alcohol to get the job done spotlessly. Remove all expansion bay pieces from the front panel of your case. These pieces will be painted individually later on.

Choosing the Paint, Primer, and Clear Coat

If you followed through with the previous two chapters and created your own window and lighting mods, you are ready to choose a paint. As you've probably noticed, a variety of spray paints are available these days, all with their own special formulas and purposes. Regular household or automotive grade spray paints are fine, and high-gloss paints can also be used.

Save Painting for Last

You should cut your case window before applying any paint; otherwise, you may have to repaint your case because of cracking and chipping caused during the cutting process.

After all the pieces are clean, it is time to choose what brand of paint, primer, and clear coat you'll use. It's a good idea to stay with the same manufacturer for all three. This means if you are using the Krylon brand of paint, for example, it is best to use a Krylon primer and clear coat as well. Doing this will often create the best results, since these paints, primers, and clear coats are matched formulaically to work together.

Sanding the Case Surface

The normal beige case, as shown in Figure 9-2, is painted using low-grade paint that was probably added during mass production. Rub your hand across the surface of your original case, and you can feel the rough bumps of the poor paint job. If you have experience in applying paint, you may know that painting a new layer on top of old and dried paint usually gives very poor results. The old paint may have rough areas that make it difficult to add a smooth second coat. To fix this small problem, you need to sand off the old paint before spraying on the new color. You may be tempted to sand all the paint off down to the bare metal, but this is not necessary; you can strip off just the top layer of the beige paint.

Figure 9-2
Unpainted beige
case surface

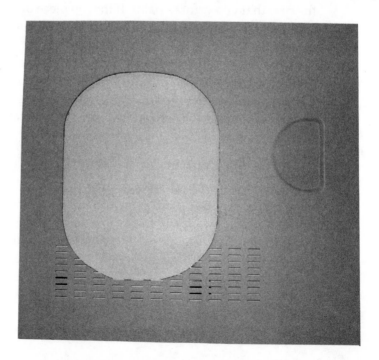

Get Rid of the Clear Coat!

The top layer of paint is often the clear coat layer that will prevent any new paint from sticking. Removing this layer is all you need to do before applying new paint to the case.

Sandpaper can be purchased at any hardware or automotive store. The many different varieties of sandpaper are categorized according to grit number (Figure 9-3), and for case work, you should pick up the wet/dry sandpaper variety. You'll find sandpaper packages with different grit ratings, which tell you how coarse the sandpaper is. The lower the grit number, the rougher the sandpaper grit. Try and find a package that includes pieces ranging from 320 to 600—this should include 320, 400, and 600 grit pieces. You may not be able to find them all in one package, so you'll have to mix and match.

Figure 9-3
Different grit
sandpaper

TIPS OF THE TRADE

How to Succeed at Sanding

Using wet/dry sandpaper allows you to use water while you're sanding. This helps prevent deep scratches from forming during the sanding process, and it cuts down on the amount of airborne paint particles.

You can sand using just the bare sheet of sandpaper, but it's a lot easier if you pick up a sanding block at the hardware store. The sandpaper can be wrapped around the block, which gives you something solid to hold onto while you are stripping away the old paint.

Pour a little water on the surface, and then move the sandpaper block in a circular motion around the areas you want sanded. Wipe down the area with a cloth between successful motions and test each sanded area with your fingers. If the area feels smooth enough and not rough, you have just completed your first sanding attempt. If you want, you can sand all the way down to the bare metal, but that's not necessary.

The front bezel or panel of your case is usually made of hard plastic. Use the 320 grit paper and slightly rough up the surface of the plastic bezel. You may want to use a 400 grit paper if the plastic is easily scarred, so test a little before you start sanding. Use the same method of sanding and wiping as you did for the metal pieces.

After the metal and plastic pieces are sanded down, clean the surface with soap and water or alcohol to remove any remaining paint particles. Let the pieces dry completely before applying the primer coat.

TWO TO THREE DAYS

Priming the Case

Priming is one of the most important steps in a great paint job. The primed layer is the glue that holds the paint to the surface—the metal case you just stripped. You do not need to prime any of the plastic parts of your case, however, as plastic will hold onto the paint easier than metal.

In general, priming and painting correctly takes time. You will need to prime and paint in separate layers, each of which requires curing between coats. During *curing*, each layer of paint is given time to dry and bond to the surface. The curing process can take several days, depending on how many layers you decide to apply.

Rust-Oleum paints, primers, and clear coats are easy to find and work fine for case painting. You can pick up Rust-Oleum paints at most hardware stores for a relatively low price. Krylon brand products are also a good choice. Figure 9-4 shows a spray can of primer.

Figure 9-4
Primer can

Before beginning, make sure that all the pieces you are priming are dry and clean. When applying primer and paint from a spray can, you should paint in an even left-to-right motion. Start spraying before you reach the surface of the case. This will prevent any heavy areas in the beginning of the paint flow, which could lead to dripping. If you miss a few places while spraying back and forth, don't worry; you will be spraying two more layers of primer on top of this one.

After the first layer has been sprayed on (Figure 9-5), let it cure for 24 hours. This will give it ample time to bond to the metal surface. If you applied the primer outdoors, move your case pieces indoors to prevent any extra airborne dust or dirt from landing on your freshly primed surface. Try not to touch any of the primed areas with your fingers, since you can leave oils from your fingers on the surface.

Figure 9-5
Initial layer applied

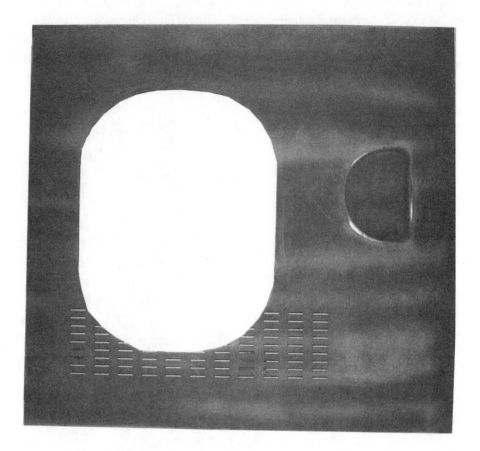

After the initial primed layer has dried, you will need to sand it again. Sanding is needed because while this layer was drying, dust or dirt particles may have fallen on it, causing bumps after the primer dried. Use water and a sheet of 400 grit sandpaper to smooth any rough edges that may have been created. Doing this before applying the second layer of primer will ensure an even and smooth coating.

Once you have sanded the rough spots, spray on the second layer as you did the first. A left-to-right spraying motion can be used, but you might opt to spray up and down this time around. Both methods will give you a good even spray in all areas. Once the second layer has been applied, let the paint dry completely for 24 hours. For the third coat, continue using the same methods of sanding and priming. A good solid surface for painting should be ready after the third layer. Sand the last layer with water and 400 grit sandpaper to give it a smooth finish. You have just primed your pieces and they're ready for painting! A fully primed side panel is shown in Figure 9-6.

Figure 9-6
Fully primed

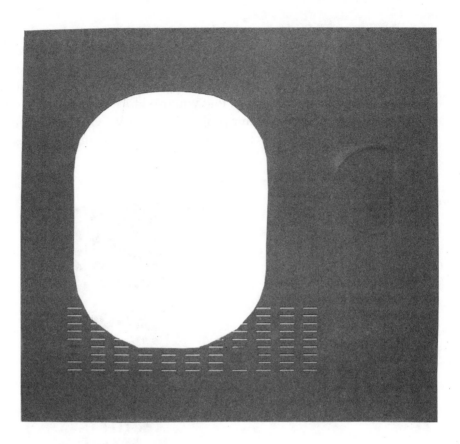

 **TWO TO THREE DAYS**   # Painting the Case

The painting method is similar to that of priming, as you are using the same layering methods. Depending on how many layers of paint you decide to use, it can take you a few days to complete this project. Three or more layers is recommended, which will give you a full and even distribution of color. Not having enough layers will cause white or dull areas to form, whereas too many layers may result in heavy areas and may cause dripping to occur.

 **TIPS OF THE TRADE**

What if I Spray too Much?

If you overspray and drips start forming, let the paint dry and then sand away the extra paint drips. This can be done over and over again until you are satisfied with the finish.

The first step to painting is prepping your work area. As explained earlier with priming, you will need to find a well-ventilated area with enough light to see where you are painting. You can select from among many paint colors, ranging from plain black to high-gloss metallic colors. Just make sure you use the same brand of paint that you used for your primer—your results will be much better for it. For this project, because we will not be creating any fancy designs, we will just cover up the whole case using glossy black spray paint, as shown in Figure 9-7.

Figure 9-7
Paint can

Using the same method you used to apply the primer, start spraying before you get to the edge of your metal piece, and spray in a left-to-right motion. This can prevent a heavy area of paint from forming in the beginning, cutting down on drips. Don't worry if you have some bare areas left over after the first pass; you will have two more chances (paint layers) to cover it up. After completing your first pass, let the paint dry. Don't go back over it. The paint will need about 24 hours to dry fully and adhere itself to the primed layer. The first painted layer is shown in Figure 9-8.

Figure 9-8
First painted layer

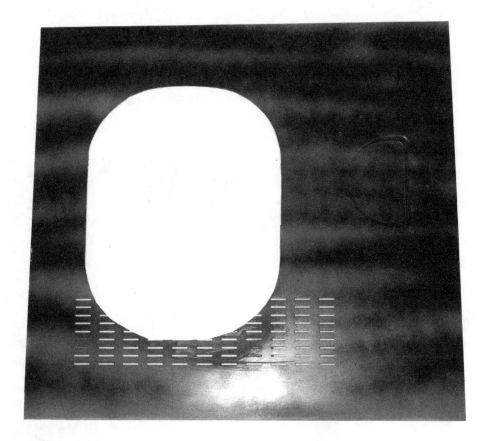

After 24 hours, take a look at your painted piece. Run your fingers over the surface, and you'll again feel some bumps and rough areas. As with the primed layer, you need to sand each of these layers to give the paint a smooth finish. Use a piece of 400 grit sandpaper to smooth out any bumps that may have formed. After sanding, wipe down the piece with a clean cloth to get rid of any debris.

Spray on the second layer using the same left-to-right method. You may also wish to flip the piece around 90 degrees—this is the up-and-down motion essentially, but you've flipped the piece to paint it more easily left to right; both methods will work in adding another layer. Once the second layer has been applied, let it dry for 24 hours.

The third layer is just like the previous two layers. Lightly sand the surface with water and 400 grit sandpaper. This should take no more than ten minutes per metal piece. Using the familiar spray procedures, apply the last layer of paint onto your case. Give it a 24-hour drying period in a dry and clean area.

After your last layer has dried completely the next day, sand it one last time before applying a clear coat. For this last sanding, you'll use a finer grit of sandpaper, because you want to remove any remaining rough spots, but you do not want to strip away the color. A 600 or higher grit will do just fine for this application, as it's less likely to scratch or scar the paint as 320 grit. After you have sanded the piece for the last time (as shown in Figure 9-9) and cleaned it thoroughly, you are ready to apply the clear coat.

Figure 9-9
Three layers of paint, fully sanded

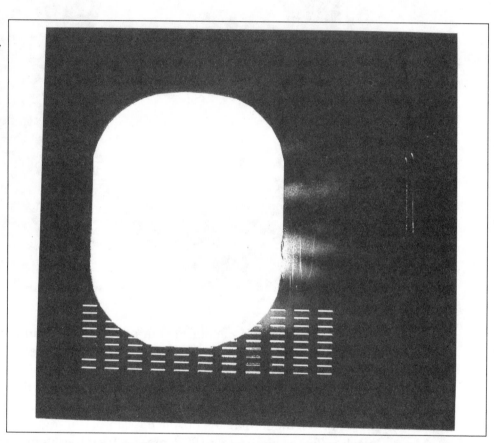

TIPS OF THE TRADE

Do Not Rush the Process!

Painting a case requires an awful lot of sanding and layering. Give yourself about a week's worth of time to complete this project. Speeding through the project will only lead to poor results.

 ## Adding Clear Coat

The last step in the painting process is applying a clear coat. The clear coat gives the painted layers a nice glossy shine and protects the painted layers from scratches by adding another thicker and harder layer on top of the three painted layers. Use a clear coat paint by the same manufacturer of the primer and paint you used (Figure 9-10). This will yield the best results in the long run.

Figure 9-10
Clear coat can

With your pieces fully painted and sanded, apply the clear coat in a left-to-right motion, again starting to spray before you hit the surface. Use a thin layer, since you will be applying three layers of clear coat. You may opt to use fewer layers if you do not want a glossy look, or you may wish to apply more to give it an even shinier look. After the initial layer of clear coat, allow 24 hours for the coat to dry and bond completely to the painted layer. Try to lay your case pieces down on a flat, horizontal surface. Propping them up vertically will promote dripping after applying the clear coat.

Before proceeding with the second layer, you can sand the dried clear coat. Some people prefer to leave it as is without sanding, but using a 600 or finer grit sandpaper to smooth it out a bit will usually make the finished surface smoother. This is up to you, as both methods will provide good results. Apply the second layer of clear coat in a left-to-right motion once again, or flip the piece around and paint in a left-to-right motion. After 24 hours of drying time, spray on the last layer. You have finished your first custom-painted case!

Finishing Up

After your third layer of clear coat has fully dried, you can apply some rubbing compound to finish up. This helps in cleaning the surface as well as blending in your new paint. If you have lightly scratched anywhere on your case, rubbing compound can help remove scratches. Wait at least 24 hours after the last clear coat before you put your case back together. You want to be careful during this time, as the paint can take up to 90 days to dry fully. Avoid dropping sharp objects on the finish during this period.

If you decide that you want to apply wax, do so after the initial 90 days. Applying wax too early can ruin your fresh paint!

Painting Optical and Floppy Drive Faceplates

After finishing the last clear coat on your painted case, you may notice something unattractive on the front panel. Your optical and floppy drives are still the same bland shade of beige! In Chapter 8, we discussed various ways to replace lights within your optical and floppy drives. You will need to apply the same techniques discussed in Chapter 8, in addition to painting the faceplates, for this segment of the project. We'll paint the drive covers of these components the same color as the case. Of course, this step is optional. If you don't mind the drives being a different color than the case, you don't have to paint them. Figure 9-11 shows painted face plate.

Figure 9-11
Painted face plate

Remove your optical drive and floppy devices if they have been reinstalled in the case. Most optical and floppy drives have removable faceplates. These can be released by pressing down on the two tabs on the left and right sides of the unit. Use a small screwdriver if you cannot release these by hand. If you are using a tray-loading device, you can manually eject the tray and remove the plastic piece at the end of the tray. They are usually hooked on, and some are glued on. Depending on the difficulty you experience trying to remove this piece, you may wish to just mask off the surrounding area and paint this small piece by itself. If you have a slot-loading optical drive, there should not be anymore parts to remove.

Follow the same case-painting precautions for your faceplates that you used with the metal pieces. Clean these plastic parts thoroughly with a clean cloth, soap and water, or alcohol. Let them dry before proceeding to the next step of the project.

Using 400 grit sandpaper, sand and rough up the surface of the faceplates. Having a little bit of a rough surface on the plastic will make it easier for the paint to adhere to it. No primer is used for these plastic parts. After a few successful strokes with the sandpaper, wipe the faceplates with a clean cloth. Lay the pieces down and use the same left-to-right motion with the spray paint. You can do this in one sweep, since the faceplate is so small.

Let the plastic piece dry overnight before spraying another layer. After a full 24 hours, check to see whether the paint has dried completely before beginning. As with the previous methods of painting, you'll sand this first layer of paint with 400 grit sandpaper. You can even use 600 grit paper if the surface does not require much sanding. After sanding, repeat the left-to-right painting sweep and let the piece sit overnight. Repeat the sanding and painting step for the third layer. Let the faceplates dry again overnight before applying the extra layers of clear coat.

HEADS UP!

Applying Enough Clear Coat Layers

One to two very thin layers of clear coat should be used on the faceplates. Keep in mind that these have to be reinstalled into their drives, so having too many layers will cause the plastic to be too thick to fit!

TWO TO THREE DAYS   ## Using Vinyl Dye

It can be difficult to keep the paint free from chips and cracks on plastic. Plastic is not an ideal painting surface because it's often porous. This can be remedied by using an alternative approach to coloring your plastic pieces. Instead of covering up your faceplate or other plastic parts with paint, you can dye them using a few sprays of vinyl dye (shown in Figure 9-12). Plastic is porous enough to soak in the thin layer of vinyl dye color. This stains the plastic instead of covering it.

Figure 9-12
Vinyl dye can

Plasti-kote is a common brand that's available in most auto shops, as it's used mainly to color vinyl surfaces in cars. One of the great advantages of using vinyl dye is that the die doesn't fill in indented or raised lettering. For example, on a CD-ROM'S faceplate, a few indented or raised letters may appear for the brand name and logo. Using vinyl dye will stain the lowered or raised surface without filling in surfaces and/or dripping. Paint, on the other hand, will create layers, causing these indents to get filled or covering up the raised lettering completely.

As you choose a dye color, think about what colors will work with your case's plastic colors. A dark-colored plastic piece will need a white vinyl dye as well as the final color dye. For example, if you decide to dye a black piece of plastic with a blue dye, and you don't first cover it in white dye, you will end up dying it a really dark tint of blue. You will not notice much change if you take this route. If you do have a dark plastic, dye the piece white before you apply the color. This will ensure a bright and clear application of the color you have chosen.

How to Prevent Vinyl Dye from Cracking

To prevent vinyl dye from cracking, make sure to keep the room temperature constant during the procedure. A large dip in temperature can cause cracking. If this happens, reapply the dye again and it should solve the problem. A temperature controlled garage will work nicely for this project.

Let's say you want to dye a 5.25-inch drive bay cover (Figure 9-13). First, clean off the surface of the plastic with a clean cloth. Use soap and water or alcohol if necessary. Place the plastic on a clean area and proceed to spray on one coat from left to right. If you have uneven and spotted areas, do not worry, because vinyl dye can take a while to stain. Give the first dye coat about 30 minutes to dry. Vinyl dye dries quickly compared to paint, but it can take 12 to 24 hours to cure. Spray on the second layer after 30 minutes and continue the process for the third coat. The beauty of using dye is that there is no need to prime or sand the plastic. There is no preparation needed and dry time is quick compared to conventional spray painting.

Figure 9-13
Dyed expansion bay

Alternative Methods

You can add some spice and color to your case in other ways. These alternatives, when applied correctly, can leave a beautiful finish on your case, but keep in mind that some of these methods may require special attention at professional facilities. This extra attention demands a higher price than your normal can of spray paint or vinyl dye. Take your time with this project and your end result will make your case stand out.

Masking and Stenciling

Instead of making a complete color change, you can mask off different designs and paint them. Stencils are also available at art supply shops, and you can use them to spray on different predefined designs. Individual letters and pictures are also available in stencil format, or you can create your own design and mask it off on your case for painting.

Painting Aluminum Cases

Aluminum cases are gaining a major hold on the computer case market. Painting these aluminum-based cases can be a lot trickier than the simple sand, prime, and paint steps described in this chapter. For aluminum cases, a step called *anodizing* can be the easy answer to this problem. Instead of painting a case a color, aluminum can be anodized by electronically depositing an oxide film on the surface of the metal. This can change the color of the aluminum as well as harden the surface—a perfect combination. This process can be completed at any metal finishing company. A search through your local yellow pages should yield a good number of locations in your area.

Using Powder Coating

Another method of coloring your case is by using powder coating. This process is usually used in the automotive industry. Powder coating is done by spraying on powder paint that is positively charged. The metal case pieces will be grounded, which will attract the powder to the surface. The powder-coated metal pieces are then placed in an oven and baked for a few minutes, causing the powder to melt. This creates an even color on the surface of the metal, and it's one of the most durable forms of coloring metal. Many road signs and bridges are powder coated to ensure durability in the harshest conditions.

**TESTING
1-2-3**

❏ Be cautious of dropping any sharp objects on the surface of your newly painted case. Within the first 90 days, the paint and all the layers above and below it may not have fully cured yet.

❏ To keep your surface shiny, you can apply some wax 90 days after you apply paint. The results are eye opening and can prolong the life of your painted project.

❏ If you decide that the color that you used on the case is not what you want, you can sand down the painted layers and reapply paint using the steps outlined in this chapter. The beauty of a personal project is that it is customizable and anything can be changed!

Index

INTERNATIONAL CONTACT INFORMATION

AUSTRALIA
McGraw-Hill Book Company Australia Pty. Ltd.
TEL +61-2-9900-1800
FAX +61-2-9878-8881
http://www.mcgraw-hill.com.au
books-it_sydney@mcgraw-hill.com

CANADA
McGraw-Hill Ryerson Ltd.
TEL +905-430-5000
FAX +905-430-5020
http://www.mcgraw-hill.ca

GREECE, MIDDLE EAST, & AFRICA
(Excluding South Africa)
McGraw-Hill Hellas
TEL +30-210-6560-990
TEL +30-210-6560-993
TEL +30-210-6560-994
FAX +30-210-6545-525

MEXICO (Also serving Latin America)
McGraw-Hill Interamericana Editores S.A. de C.V.
TEL +525-117-1583
FAX +525-117-1589
http://www.mcgraw-hill.com.mx
fernando_castellanos@mcgraw-hill.com

SINGAPORE (Serving Asia)
McGraw-Hill Book Company
TEL +65-6863-1580
FAX +65-6862-3354
http://www.mcgraw-hill.com.sg
mghasia@mcgraw-hill.com

SOUTH AFRICA
McGraw-Hill South Africa
TEL +27-11-622-7512
FAX +27-11-622-9045
robyn_swanepoel@mcgraw-hill.com

SPAIN
McGraw-Hill/Interamericana de España, S.A.U.
TEL +34-91-180-3000
FAX +34-91-372-8513
http://www.mcgraw-hill.es
professional@mcgraw-hill.es

UNITED KINGDOM, NORTHERN,
EASTERN, & CENTRAL EUROPE
McGraw-Hill Education Europe
TEL +44-1-628-502500
FAX +44-1-628-770224
http://www.mcgraw-hill.co.uk
computing_europe@mcgraw-hill.com

ALL OTHER INQUIRIES Contact:
McGraw-Hill/Osborne
TEL +1-510-596-6600
FAX +1-510-596-7600
http://www.osborne.com
omg_international@mcgraw-hill.com